Writing and Society: An Introduction

How does writing relate to speech? What impact does it have on social organization and development? How do unwritten languages differ from those that have a written form and tradition? This book is a general account of the place of writing in society. Drawing on contemporary and historical examples, from clay tablets to touch-screen displays, the book explores the functions of writing and written language, analysing their consequences for language, society, economy and politics. It examines the social causes of illiteracy, demonstrating that institutions of central importance to modern society are built upon writing and written texts, and are characterized by specific forms of communication. It explores the social dimensions of spelling and writing reform, as well as of digital literacy, a new mode of expression and communication posing novel challenges to the student of language in society.

FLORIAN COULMAS is Director of the German Institute for Japanese Studies (DIJ) in Tokyo.

D1353735

KEY TOPICS IN SOCIOLINGUISTICS

Series editor: Rajend Mesthrie

This new series focusses on the main topics of study in sociolinguistics today. It consists of accessible yet challenging accounts of the most important issues to consider when examining the relationship between language and society. Some topics have been the subject of sociolinguistic study for many years, and are here re-examined in the light of new developments in the field; others are issues of growing importance that have not so far been given a sustained treatment. Written by leading experts, the books in the series are designed to be used on courses and in seminars, and include useful suggestions for further reading and a helpful glossary.

Already published in the series:

Politeness by Richard J. Watts

Language Policy by Bernard Spolsky

Discourse by Jan Blommaert

Analyzing Sociolinguistic Variation by Sali A. Tagliamonte

Language and Ethnicity by Carmen Fought

Style by Nikolas Coupland

World Englishes by Rajend Mesthrie and Rakesh Bhatt

Language and Identity by John Edwards

Attitudes to Language by Peter Garrett

Language Attrition by Monika S. Schmid

Forthcoming titles:

Sociolinguistic Fieldwork by Natalie Schilling

Writing and Society

An Introduction

FLORIAN COULMAS

CAMBRIDGE UNIVERSITY PRESS
Cambridge, New York, Melbourne, Madrid, Cape Town,
Singapore, São Paulo, Delhi, Mexico City

Cambridge University Press
The Edinburgh Building, Cambridge CB2 8RU, UK

Published in the United States of America by Cambridge University Press, New York

www.cambridge.org
Information on this title: www.cambridge.org/9781107602434

First published 2013

Printed and bound in the United Kingdom by the MPG Books Group

A catalogue record for this publication is available from the British Library

Library of Congress Cataloguing in Publication data
Coulmas, Florian, author.
Writing and Society : An Introduction / Florian Coulmas.
pages   cm. – (Key topics in sociolinguistics)
Includes bibliographical references and index.
ISBN 978-1-107-01642-2 (hardback)
1. Writing   Social aspects.   2. Written communication   Social aspects.
3. Literacy   Social aspects.   I. Title.
P211.7.C69   2012
302.2′244 – dc23   2012022015

ISBN 978-1-107-01642-2 Hardback
ISBN 978-1-107-60243-4 Paperback

Contents

Illustrations

Tables

Preface

Writing systems and written language are objects of great complexity and wonder testifying to human ingenuity and the determination to create our own universe. If language is the most distinctive inborn trait of our species, writing is our most consequential invention. It is so ubiquitous in everyday life that one has to wonder what purposes it serves. How does writing relate to speech? What impact does it have on social organization and development? How do unwritten languages differ from those that have a written form and tradition? In twentieth-century linguistics it has been axiomatic that writing is unimportant, but this is hardly so, certainly not if we direct our attention to the social aspects of language behaviour, a society's repertoire of codes, and the division of labour between different modes of linguistic communication. From a sociological point of view the very concept of a language, in the sense of one language being distinct from another, is indissolubly bound up with writing. If we want to understand the social functions of language, both speech and writing must be taken into consideration, as well as the multifaceted interplay of the two.

In this little book I have recorded my observations and thoughts about the role written language and writing play in society. For historical reasons explained in the first chapter sociolinguistics has not been very interested in or accommodating to writing. However, nowadays, not just Trappist monks but many other younger tribes write more than they speak and writing has evolved from a specialized skill into a mass mode of communication. The communicatively relevant parts of social environments can no longer be adequately described and analysed unless writing is recognized as a crucial component of linguistic ecology. The reasons for this are less theoretical than empirical. Humanity has moved steadily towards relying on written communication in ever more domains of life. This involves changes in communicative behaviour, in language socialization, in the ways we learn and acquire knowledge, and in the formation and maintaining of social networks. The media revolution is not just a catchword; it is a reality to which we are forced to adapt and in which writing is of central importance. Many of the on-going changes we are only beginning to understand. This book, therefore, rather than summing-up the results of a consolidated field of research should be seen as offering a perspective on the emergent subject area of writing in society.

Acknowledgements

Chapter 2, 'The past in the present and the seeds of the public sphere', overlaps with a chapter I contributed to *Linguistic Landscape: Expanding the Scenery*, edited by Elana Shohamy and Durk Gorter (London: Routledge, 2009), pp. 13–24. In Chapters 4 and 6, 'Literacy and inequality' and 'Writing reform,' respectively, I have used several sections of a paper I wrote jointly with Federica Guerini, entitled 'Literacy and writing reform' which appeared in *The Cambridge Handbook of Language Policy*, edited by Bernard Spolsky (Cambridge University Press, 2012), pp. 437–60. And Chapter 5, 'The society of letters,' draws on material contained in my article 'Social practices of speech and writing,' published in *The Cambridge Encyclopedia of the Language Sciences*, edited by Patrick C. Hogan (Cambridge University Press, 2011), pp. 35–45. I am grateful to acknowledge the publishers' permission to use these materials.

I want to thank Tessa Carroll who read the entire manuscript, which benefited very much from her comments and useful suggestions. Special thanks are due to Claus Harmer who helped me with some of the illustrations.

1 The tyranny of writing and the dominance of vernacular speech

We live in a literate world. This is true, notwithstanding the fact, that according to UNESCO statistics, there were, in 2010, some 790 million illiterate adults in the world, more than the population of the European Union. However, even in the African and Asian countries where illiterate adults are concentrated, oral culture is no longer considered a viable alternative to literate culture – a different way of life, a matter of preference that could be sustained. Life without letters is a paradise lost, if a paradise it was. In our day and age, reading and writing are indispensable for participation in society, and there is no evading the fact that literacy skills are a major determinant of one's life chances. This holds for the world at large and is even less debatable for industrialized countries. Illiteracy in these countries is a deplorable state of affairs, a social injustice that excludes a small minority from mainstream society. Language in the written mode is part of everyone's everyday communication behaviour, actively and passively and, in the case of the illiterate, confronts them with an insurmountable barrier. It is, therefore, argued nowadays that literacy is a universal human right.[1]

Writing has been around for at least five millennia, and although universal literacy is a recent achievement in only some parts of the world, writing has exercised an influence on language for a long time. In fact, a clear distinction between writing and language has not always been made, neither in everyday discourse nor in scholarship. It is perhaps understandable, therefore, that, in order to eliminate confusion and to establish the object proper of linguistic inquiry, modern linguists have emphasized speech, relegating writing to the sidelines. Linguistics, it has been argued repeatedly, should study *natural* language – that is, the inborn capacity for language – and while human beings are born to speak, they are not born to write. This is the basis of the argument for the neglect of writing in linguistics. A brief review of the origin of this argument is useful in order to appreciate its merits and the influence it had on theory formation in linguistics as well as in sociolinguistics.

1

The argument can be traced back to two influential founders of structural linguistics, Ferdinand de Saussure and Leonard Bloomfield. These two scholars, each for his own reasons concerned with laying the foundations of a synchronic linguistics as opposed to historical philology, made a strong case for abstracting, in the scientific study of language, away from writing.

SAUSSURE'S ARGUMENT AGAINST WRITING

One of Saussure's lasting achievements was to establish the science of speech sounds as the cornerstone of structural linguistics. Chapter 7 of his *Course in General Linguistics*, on phonology, begins with a most vivid metaphor: 'Whoever consciously deprives himself of the perceptible image of the written word runs the risk of perceiving only a shapeless and unmanageable mass. Taking away the written form is like depriving a beginning swimmer of his life belt' (Saussure 1978: 32). However, it was exactly this that he felt was necessary to achieve his objective of coming to grips with the structure he knew was inherent in the 'shapeless and unmanageable mass' in a way that was not compromised and distorted by the imperfect graphic rendition of speech sounds. He had to make the case that linguists should indeed jump into the deep, without the lifebelt of writing. Citing the example of the name of the French town *Auch* which is pronounced [ɔːʃ], he denounced 'the tyranny of writing' and said that 'orthography is unimportant' (1978: 31). It was in this context that Saussure lamented the fact that spelling influences and modifies language. His concern was to make sure that linguists would study what they meant to study, rather than a distorted image thereof.

Saussure had a point, for lettered people like him, unless they are trained linguists, tend both to attribute more importance to the permanent and stable written word than to what Anthony Burgess (1992) called 'a mouthful of air', and to conceptualize language in terms of the visual images of its units. It is by means of books, dictionaries and grammars that proper language is taught and raised onto the level of conscious reflection. The fact Saussure saw very clearly is that the perception of language is heavily influenced by writing. A naïve understanding of the Latin alphabet as a writing system that is (ideally) grounded in a one-to-one correspondence between letters and sounds reinforces the tendency to conflate the distinction between the two. Saussure was concerned, and rightly so, that writing obscures our view of language, an entirely abstract system of values, and that we must exclude it from the analysis of language because it 'is unrelated to its inner system' (1978:

23). He thus concluded that 'the linguistic object is not both the written and the spoken forms of words: the spoken forms alone constitute the object' (1978: 23f.).

Saussure's emphasis on speech as the primary manifestation of language and his insistence that linguistic analysis must be concerned with abstract units and relationships rather than physical manifestations were well reasoned and proved to be very influential for linguistic theory formation and beyond, laying the groundwork of Structuralism. Yet his argument about writing was flawed. The first flaw concerns his assertion, quoted above, that writing is unrelated to the inner system of language. Without going into the details of what the inner system of language is, it can be said that, unless writing were a graphic code entirely of its own, it must be related to the inner system of language in one way or another; otherwise, it could not be interpreted in linguistic terms, which, however, seems to be the very point. Writing must be readable, and that means interpretable on the basis of more or less systematic mapping relations between sound, meaning and graphic sign within the framework of a given language. However deficient and convoluted, writing thus does relate to the inner system of language.

The second flaw of Saussure's argument for excluding writing from linguistics is of a somewhat different quality. He acknowledged the influence of writing on our perception of language and hence, ultimately, on language itself. He also allowed for the possibility that 'writing may retard the process of [language] change under certain conditions' (1978: 24), but saw this as an aberration that should be disregarded, an artefact that disrupts the natural course of events. In his understanding, language was a natural faculty, and it was the linguist's task to discover the 'precise laws [that] govern its evolution' (1978: 31). The scientification of the study of language was his project. Natural laws rather than the vagaries of human life were to him what could best, and therefore should, explain the reality of language. His observation that 'when there is disagreement between language and orthography . . . the written form almost inevitably wins out' (1978: 25), rather than furnishing the motivation for studying the interaction between speech, writing and language, led him to the conclusion that 'writing assumes undeserved importance' (1978: 25) and should thus be disregarded. In retrospect this is not a little surprising, for, much as he was concerned with laying the foundations of linguistics as an exact science, Saussure also emphasized that language is 'a social fact' (1978: 6), 'a social institution' (1978: 15). What this meant must be discussed in detail.

Saussure was quite aware of the tension inherent in characterizing language as both a *natural* faculty – subject to natural laws – and a *social*

institution – subject to man-made rules and conventions. He compared
language to other institutions such as political and legal institutions
which, by virtue of being sign systems, share important properties with
language. However, language, he argued, is a social institution unlike
any other, because: (1) it involves all members of the relevant community all the time, and (2) it cannot be changed at will. Thus, while
language is a collective product, artificial interventions cannot alter
the course of its evolution. The discovery in the nineteenth century that
sound change is systematic and follows inalterable rules lent credence
to Saussure's argument and the exclusion of writing from the study of
language it implied.

BLOOMFIELD'S ARGUMENT AGAINST WRITING

Like Saussure, Bloomfield conceived of language as an institution
and considered the study of linguistic change essential 'because it
offers the only possibility of explaining the phenomenon of language'
(Bloomfield 1933: 281). Language change is continuous, a fact that is
often overlooked because (1) the speed of change is slow, and (2) writing
suggests stability. Moreover, those dealing with language profession-
ally are biased towards writing, for 'we today are so used to reading
and writing that we often confuse these activities with language itself'
(1933: 283). This is an impediment to analytic insight because 'the conventions of writing remain unaltered even though the speech-forms
have undergone linguistic change' (1933: 292). Since linguistic change
proceeds regardless of whether and how writing conventions change,
written records cannot, without much careful interpretation, serve as
data. They are as Bloomfield (1933: 21) put it, 'a handicap' to the study
of language.

Another point that Bloomfield adduced is that writing is a recent
invention that has 'been in use for any considerable length of time in
only a few speech-communities . . . confined to a very few persons' (1933:
282). His observation that 'all languages were spoken through nearly all
of their history by people who did not read or write' (1933: 21) is incon-
trovertible. It provided for him a reason to assert the primacy of ordinary
spoken language over written texts as a subject for linguistic analysis.
Yet the influence of writing on speech is something he could not ignore.
Again like Saussure, he took issue with discrepancies between spoken
and written forms and assumed that, in this event, 'people are likely
to infer that there exists a preferable variant that matches the written
form', adding, 'especially, it would seem, in the last centuries with the

spread of literacy' (1933: 487). He commented on the pervasiveness in some languages of 'bookish borrowings' which often do not conform with the sound change patterns of other parts of the lexicon. He furthermore remarked that 'a *literary dialect* may become established and obligatory for written records, regardless of the writer's actual dialect' (1933: 292).

The two founding fathers of structural linguistics felt they had to resist the 'tyranny of writing' to make the case for a linguistics that investigates language regardless of whether it has a written form, and to make sure that writing did not interfere with the study of language in an uncontrolled and hence unwelcome way, for their predecessors often 'failed to distinguish between letters and sounds' (Saussure 1978: 24). What is more, both scholars realized that unwritten languages were deserving of the linguist's attention no less than those with a long literary tradition, a point of particular importance to Bloomfield, who took an interest in native American languages that had never been recorded or used in writing. Their advice was sound, important for the development of linguistic theory, and hugely influential; however, it led to the baby of writing being thrown out with the bath water of its messy effects on linguistic analysis. Given the attention Saussure and Bloomfield paid to writing in their seminal books, it would seem doubtful that this is what they intended. Neither of them denied the influence in literate societies of writing on language, but it was not what they meant to study. Following their lead, theoretical linguistics saw the emergence of research paradigms that have no place for writing.

Bloomfield's (1933: 21) statement that 'writing is not language, but merely a way of recording language by means of visible marks' belongs to the stock-quotations cited in linguistics textbooks. Excluding writing from the objects of investigation became all but a defining feature of linguistics. Today, the priority of spoken over written language is generally accepted in linguistics, and understandably so.

Lyons (1968), writing a generation after Bloomfield, still had some thoughtful observations about the relative independence of written and spoken language in some languages such as French and Chinese, differences of grammatical structure and vocabulary that distinguish the spontaneously acquired from the learned language. Lyons (1968: 41) also mentioned 'the peculiar status of Latin in medieval and Renaissance Europe' which, he said, tended to confirm the principle of the priority of the written language. These facts, however, did not persuade him or generations of students who came to linguistics by studying his deservedly influential textbook to abandon or even modify the principle of the priority of the spoken language. Lyons still felt that he had to argue

Saussure's case that linguistics from a synchronic point of view ought to deal with speech rather than writing. Since then, this has become taken for granted. Introductions to linguistics usually have little to say about writing and written language. Some of the more widely used textbooks, such as Radford *et al.* (1999), Fromkin (2000) and Matthews (2003) have no chapter on writing; others, such as Poole (1999) and O'Grady, Dobrovosky and Karanba (1997), include a final chapter about writing systems that is likely to be skipped at the end of the course. In this sense, the tyranny of writing has been successfully defeated, vernacular speech being universally recognized as the legitimate object of linguistic study.

ARE SAUSSURE'S AND BLOOMFIELD'S ARGUMENTS STILL VALID?

Saussure and Bloomfield argued against (1) the confusion of writing with language, and (2) the elements of writing entering into the process of linguistic description. Both points are valid, but they have been taken to heart only partially.[2] The most widely used linguistic transcription system, the International Phonetic Alphabet (IPA), is an offshoot of the Latin alphabet. It was first designed in the 1880s in France by 'Dhi Fonètik Tîcerz' Asóciécon' (The Phonetic Teachers' Association) as a tool for transcribing the sounds of foreign languages, and has been revised and undoubtedly improved many times since, by adding letters for sounds not present in European languages and providing for other phonetic differentiations. But the basic principle of *writing* is still the same. For the purposes of analysis the stream of speech sounds, which is a continuum, is divided into discrete units that only in a very abstract sense correspond to something in the empirical reality of speech. The visualization of speech by means of an IPA transcription produces an inappropriate picture suggesting that speech is something discontinuous, consisting of distinct and discrete elements. By using the IPA, linguists thus create the object of their investigation. This is by no means a minor technicality. Assuming some kind of equivalence between an extent in time – speech – and an extent in space – writing – is no less problematic in linguistics than in physics, where it is at the heart of the question of permanence and change and our understanding of the universe. However, short of solving the mystery of the continuity of space-time, linguistics cannot but approach the nature of language by constructing models of it. Writing systems, including the IPA, can be understood in this sense as models of language.

Linguistics as Saussure conceived it is not an empirical science, such as, for example, mineralogy, which studies the physical properties of minerals found in the environment, produces taxonomies, and on that basis develops theories about their origin and formation. By contrast, phonemes and other units of language, such as syllables, morphemes, words, sentences and meanings, cannot be observed in the environment, being theoretical constructs. Knowledge generation in linguistics thus proceeds in the opposite direction from those natural sciences that start out from evidence gathered via sense experience. In the field of language, there are no given observable objects to start out with, because speech communities are not uniform, and no two people speak exactly alike. In fact, no one speaker speaks exactly the same on different occasions. Linguists, therefore, have to deal with an 'unmanageable mass', as Saussure called it; and to get a grip on it, they make assumptions about it and impose upon it structures, whose plausibility can be assessed, both internally as being more or less consistent (free of contradictions, redundancies and ad hoc rationalizations), and externally on the basis of speakers' judgements about similarities and differences. As we have seen above, Saussure and Bloomfield realized the influence of writing on people's speech behaviour and perception of language. Since linguistics, to establish its object of investigation, depends on speakers' judgements, it cannot very well ignore this kind of influence, simply on the grounds that language would evolve no matter whether it is or is not used in writing. If for that reason alone, writing must therefore be taken into account in the study of language in literate speech communities. Bloomfield's pronouncement that 'in order to study writing, we must know something about language, but the reverse is not true' (1933: 21) was useful at a time when the study of unwritten languages needed justification. Nowadays it can no longer guide us, for there are many things about language we cannot understand without studying its written form: the writing system, the effect of written norms, writing-mediated language contact, and language attitudes, for example. The invention of writing, although it occurred relatively recently in the history of the human species, has revolutionized the way language can be used. Writing may well be adaptive, for example, by being conducive to co-operative behaviour in a range beyond earshot. This aspect of the nature–culture interplay that characterizes human language must be recognized.

As Saussure said, language has both a natural and a social/cultural side, and while it is perhaps impossible to change sound laws deliberately, other aspects of language are open to intentional modification and innovation. Clearly, the written form of language is entirely on the sociocultural side, but if there are distinct written varieties, and if it is the case, as Saussure and Bloomfield assert, that these varieties have a bearing on linguistic change, writing must not be ignored. For, unless we reflect on the nature of the relationship between linguistic units and their graphic representation and unless we remember that the IPA is derived from the Latin alphabet and not vice versa, we are ill equipped to avoid the trap into which Saussure and Bloomfield accused their predecessors of having fallen. Conventional writing is not language, true; but graphical renditions of speech by means of the IPA or any other notation system are not language either.

THE SOCIAL INDEXICALITY OF LINGUISTIC RESOURCES

How did the tyranny of writing come about, and why is it so entrenched? One of two answers to this question has to do with the medium and our senses, and the other has to do with power. 'Seeing is believing' says the proverb. Demonstrative evidence is convincing to us, and of all our senses, even though it is the most easily deceived, it is our sight that we trust most. This might be seen as testimony to the immense importance of vision in human life, survival and adaptation to the environment, which, perhaps, also makes us attribute more importance to the written than to the spoken word.

In addition to evolutionary reasons underlying our inclination to rely on vision, the 'undeserved importance' of writing stems from the fact that knowledge of the written language has never been, and is not still, distributed evenly in society. Rather, literacy skills are indicative of social status and prestige and they correlate with other social variables. The acquisition of writing by a speech community produces an unprecedented and irreversible alteration in its communicative resources and their functional allocation. In all societies writing is associated with authority, that is, with an *auctor* – whence 'author' – one who sets forth written statements and is empowered to enforce obedience. In this sense, the 'tyranny' of writing is a social reality that ought to be studied as such. In literate societies, most speakers and listeners are also readers and writers whose linguistic repertoire is shaped not just by the input received through the auditory channel, but also from the linguistic landscape in which they grow up and the written texts they are exposed to from an early age, as well as by the school that functions as an agent for the legitimization and reproduction of an official or national language. While it is true that 'all languages were spoken through most of their history by people who did not read and write', today most people do read and write and the most widely spoken languages have a long literary tradition. The remaining unwritten languages are many, but their speakers are few, and many of them are literate in another language.

When language is studied from the point of view of its social nature, including the uses that society makes of its linguistic resources, there is every reason to consider both its spoken and its written forms, which vary along stylistic scales of formality and context dependence as well as in terms of attitudes and potential for social regulation. For sociologists interested in language – there aren't all that many – it would make little sense to exclude writing from their field of inquiry. To them the 'tyranny of writing' that Saussure noted is a prime reason for studying it, for it is testimony to the great importance of writing in society. While mainstream sociology has paid scant attention to writing, it must be noted that some of the most influential contemporary thinkers, notably Habermas and Derrida, put writing at the centre of their philosophy. Habermas built in his early work a media and communication theory of the public sphere to which we will return in Chapter 2. To him the distinction between speech and writing corresponds to that between the naïve participant in communicative interaction and the reflecting observer of discourse (Habermas 2008). Derrida (1967) has presented powerful arguments against the reductionist view of writing as a mere expression of speech, maintaining instead that in order to understand the development of language the interplay between speech and writing must be studied. Only by abandoning de Saussure's tenet of the secondary nature of writing as a supplement to speech can the true symbolic power of writing be appreciated. It lies in the fact that writing expands the range of intellectual pursuits beyond what is possible without it. Examples cited by Derrida (1972) include sign systems such as theoretical mathematics and information retrieval systems that have never been absolutely linked with phonetic language production. Their existence and the effects they can have on speech and language suggest that speech and writing, although related in rule-governed ways, are autonomous systems that, once writing has been created, develop and mutually influence each other. For the purposes of this book, the autonomy of writing is a more promising starting point than the notion that writing is derived from and secondary to speech.

Another important thinker who paid much attention to the symbolic power of language was the French sociologist Bourdieu. In order to understand the social functioning of language, the differences between situated speech and language as a regulated, normative system imposed on a community must be analysed. Linguists, Bourdieu notes, tacitly accept 'the *official* definition of the *official* language' when they speak, as they tend to do, of 'the language' without further qualification (Bourdieu 1991: 45). The crucial importance of writing in this connection is obvious, for the language in question, which Bourdieu calls the legitimate or 'authorized language', is 'produced by authors who have the authority to write' and it is 'fixed and codified by grammarians . . . [as] a system of norms regulating linguistic practices' (1991: 45). Bourdieu's 'linguistic practices' can be linked easily with Basil Bernstein's notion of class-specific codes, which will be discussed below. Both concepts can be understood as habitual systems of meaning that represent symbolic resources and serve, among other things, social reproduction, including the reproduction of inequality. As a social practice, writing occupies a different position in the symbolic resources of different societies and is charged with different functions relating to power in different ways. From a sociological point of view, it is plainly evident that, rather than serving as a substitute for speech, writing constitutes a part of a society's communication apparatus that is not derived from speech and cannot be replaced by speech. It is a social practice and a mode of communication in its own right.

However, the appreciation of writing in social philosophy had little impact on mainstream sociolinguistics. Influenced by structural linguistics of the Saussurean or Bloomfieldian strands, mainstream sociolinguistics has by and large ignored writing, focussing on vernacular speech instead. The rationale for restricting the object of investigation in this way is that vernacular speech is most spontaneous and least monitored consciously by its speakers. For this reason it is said to be the variety sociolinguists should study, because it provides them with 'the most systematic data for the analysis of linguistic structure' (Labov 1972: 208). Labov's insistence on spontaneity as a criterion for selecting a speech style suitable for data collection echoes Saussure's condemnation of the tyranny of writing, which has thus been replaced by the dominance of the vernacular. However, if, as I have argued elsewhere (Coulmas 2005) and as most sociolinguists agree, language behaviour is under all circumstances a matter of choice, it is not really plausible that, for the purpose of data collection, varieties characterized by a higher degree of conscious monitoring than vernacular speech should be sidestepped, for the extent to which the choice of vocabulary, style and pronunciation is conscious and guided by orientation to a norm, real or imagined, is socially indicative. What is more, language is the tool that humans employ if not for cognition, then certainly for communicating its results to others. Why the conscious monitoring of using and thereby shaping this tool should get in the way of understanding how it works remains an enigma.

Different members of a speech community use their linguistic resources differently. Some of the differences are individual and others social, concerning social networks, stratification, level of education, gender, minority status, etc., as well as attitudes towards speech styles. Some styles are highly regarded, others looked down upon, and these distinctions correlate with the perceived and actual social status of their speakers. Writing has a strong bearing on these distinctions. In this, connection, Kahane introduced the notion of 'the prestige language', that which is written – that is: 'In literate societies, one of the primary MOTIVATIONS for acquiring the prestige language is its identification with education, which transfers to it the values of a class symbol' (Kahane 1986: 495). Similarly, Bloomfield's term 'literary dialect', quoted above, provides a descriptive catchword for the social indexicality of a distinct variety that is characterized first and foremost by being associated with writing.

ELABORATING THE LITERARY DIALECT

Once available in a society, writing can no longer be ignored, and with the spread of literacy, as Bloomfield noted, its influence increases not only by making available an additional channel of communication, but also by expanding and differentiating the range of verbal expression. You can talk like a book only if you have a book. Among the first to recognize the social significance of differential access to communicative resources was Basil Bernstein, who built on it an elaborate theory of language and the perpetuation of social class in industrial society.

Bernstein identified two general types of linguistic codes or systems of meaning, *elaborated* codes and *restricted* codes, which he understood as a function of particular forms of social relationships and qualities of social structure (Bernstein 1966). Restricted codes are highly dependent on context and situation, redundant, oriented towards social relations, and intertwined with nonverbal communication, whereas elaborated codes are geared to verbalizing precise meanings and individual intent, and are not indexed to the here and now. Predictability of syntax and lexicon is high in a restricted code and low in an elaborated code. Restricted and elaborated codes differ in terms of verbal planning and the interlocutors' orientation towards each other. The co-presence of speaker and listener is characteristic of restricted speech forms in which reference is frequently exophoric (outside the text), relying to a large extent on the shared situational setting. Compared with that, referent identification in elaborated speech forms is made verbally explicit and in this sense freed from the speech situation. Restricted codes are used by all speakers. They include routinized patterns of speech in rituals and other recurrent situations in which little variation is expected or tolerated, as well as intimate talk that relies on a great deal of shared knowledge. Using restricted codes is not necessarily indicative of social class; being largely confined in one's communication behaviour to a restricted code is, for lack of choice between different codes is strongly indicative of a low or deficient level of education.

Bernstein observed that middle-class children differed from working-class children in their lexical and syntactic choices, the former exhibiting a higher frequency of elaborated code features than the latter. His interest in the cognitive orientations and modes of language use he called codes was in their being related to the socioeconomic background of speakers and hearers. Much like Bourdieu (1982), he recognized language not as a mere reflection of society, but as a contributing element in the construction and perpetuation of the social order. His sociological theory of language codes met with various criticisms – for example: for confounding stylistic variation – plain vs formal – with variation in messages – simple vs complex (O'Keef and Delia 1988); for distinguishing only two modes of functioning in verbal communication, a restricted code and an elaborated code, related to two social strata, working-class and middle-class (Philipsen 1997); and for being conducive to a view of working-class speech as deficient (Danzig 1995).[3] However, since it is still being referred to as a major contribution to understanding the functioning of language in society, Bernstein's model has in many ways stood the test of time.

The originality of Bernstein's analysis of differential speech patterns was to link them to different learning styles and social identities: 'As a child learns an elaborated code he learns . . . to orient towards the verbal channel . . . He comes to perceive language as a set of theoretical possibilities for the presentation of his discrete experience to others' (Bernstein 1966: 257). In contrast, for a child who is limited to a restricted code, 'speech does not become the object of special perceptual activity, neither does a theoretical attitude develop towards the structural possibilities of sentence organization' (1966: 258). In his later work, Bernstein refined and developed the notions of restricted and elaborated codes, assigning them a central position in his theory of social order and its reproduction. For present purposes, his initial, rather crude, descriptions are still relevant. If we consider the contrast between the speaker of an elaborated code who *perceives language as a set of theoretical possibilities for the presentation of his discrete experience to others* and a user of a restricted code who *does not develop a theoretical attitude towards the structural possibilities*

of sentence organization, it becomes apparent that the different percep-
tions of language characteristic of the two codes correspond to those
associated with writing and spontaneous speech, respectively. Typically,
writing involves careful planning, conscious selection of the theoretical
possibilities the language provides, and the presentation of an experience or state of affairs to others in such a way that they can understand
it on the basis of the written words alone. Writers need to be clear and
explicit, for their readers may not share their co-ordinates, their time,
place and point of view. In spontaneous speech we can afford to be
sloppy, or rather, implicit, relying on the physical presence of, and the
shared knowledge with, our interlocutors. Ong spelt out the close connection between written language and elaborated code most explicitly:
'The elaborated code is one which is formed with the necessary aid of
writing, and, for full elaboration, of print' (Ong 1982: 105). Consider two
examples:

1   Composed text

Convergence or frontal lifting takes place when two masses of air come
together. In most cases, the two air masses have different temperature and
moisture characteristics. One of the air masses is usually warm and moist,
while the other is cold and dry. The leading edge of the latter air mass acts as
an inclined wall or front causing the moist warm air to be lifted. Of course the
lifting causes the warm moist air mass to cool due to expansion resulting in
saturation. This cloud formation mechanism is common at the mid-latitudes
where cyclones form along the polar front and near the equator where the
trade winds meet at the intertropical convergence zone.

Tropical cyclones are regarded as a subtype of the 'Mesoscale Convective
System'. They differ from the other cloud vortex forms by having other emerge,
development and structure. They are frontless low pressure systems with
organized convection, heavy thunderstorms and a closed surface-wind
circulation around the low pressure centre. They are also well-known as
Hurricanes or Typhoons. The sizes of the cyclone are from 500–700 km to 1200,
rare 1500km. Its cloud top height reaches 12–15, to 16 km. The albedo is 0.8–1.[4]

2   Spontaneous conversation

1 Mel: Tom Barry got a:ll that- (0.2) stuff off to (0.3)
2 Liz: Did ↑ee?=
3 Mel: =th' schoo:l. °Yea:h. ( ).°=
5 Liz: =An: so he wor- managed ta make it wo:rk. (0.8)
6 Mel: Yeah-. (0.5)
7 Liz: °W'll° ↓there you ↑go:. (2.1)
8 Mel: °Mm- There ya go°.=
9 Liz: =Ho:w long d't ta:ke 'im. (2.9)
10 Mel: A::h;= °nod 'll tha-t lo:ng°, (7.3)
11 Mel: Very clever ma:n;= is To:m¿ (1.3)
12 Liz: ↑How o:ld ↓is he. (2.5)
13 Mel: Don'know;= ee'd be: late ↑twenties:¿ ↓early ↑thirdies¿ (1.0)

14 Liz: He needs a hai:rcut. (2.2)
15 Mel: He:'s a (0.7) hippy:;= ↓fr'm the sevendies. (0.4)
16 Liz: Doesn' he kno:w¿= th't it's ni:nedee:n ni:nedy o:ne?=
17 Mel: =Hehh (0.3) ·HHUH
18 Liz: ↑'x↑↑tra:wrdinry.
19 Mel: °°Yehh°°. (Gardner, Fitzgerald and Mushin 2009: 76f.)[5]

The explanation of the meteorological properties of cloud formation in the first example would be most unlikely to be produced in spontaneous speech. Complete sentences follow one upon the other without hesitation, repetition, false starts, incomplete chunks of phrasal units, fillers, contracted forms, ellipsis and other features of conversational speech. No expressions of temporal and spatial deixis tie the text to a particular situation. It is autonomous, relying on the words, including some technical vocabulary, and the rules of English grammar alone. In contrast to this, the second example exhibits many of the typical features of conversational speech, such as exophoric reference (*all that stuff*), false starts (*so he wor- .. managed to make it work*), conversational routine formulae with phatic rather than content function (*well there you go, mm there ya go*), and many long pauses. The syntax is simple, containing no subordinate clauses. The subject of the conversation between Mel and Liz is Tom Barry. What they say about him is not hard to understand, although it remains unclear what Tom managed to make work. Mel and Liz evidently know and thus need not 'spell' it out explicitly. They are intimates and can rely both on shared knowledge and on a common conversational history. Most of their utterances make sense only in the context of the on-going conversation.

WRITING AND ELABORATED CODE

The distinction between restricted and elaborated codes is not the same as that between speech and writing, but it is clear that the former has similarities with face-to-face speech, while the latter shares the characteristics of decontextualized texts. Both writing and speech are used in various different ways, and written messages can be highly contextual manifesting a restricted code. A Post-it note on the office door, 'Back in 5 minutes', does not represent a very elaborate code. The medium is not all-determining; rather, the point to emphasize here is that developing a highly elaborated code is furthered by, if not dependent on, the practice of reading and writing which involves a language use very different from face-to-face communication. Being interested in explaining the difference in scholastic performance between working-class and middle-class children, Bernstein theorized that the elaborated code of verbal explicitness is characteristic of both the middle-class – households with books – and the school setting, thus affording middle-class children an advantage. 'The relative backwardness of lower working class and rural children', he concluded, 'may well be a form of culturally induced backwardness' built into the social system, for 'the code the child brings to the school symbolizes his social identity' (Bernstein 1966: 259).

Bernstein's was a sociological argument, presenting codes as a function of social hierarchy. His interest in the relationship between code and social class provided a strong impulse for the early development of sociolinguistic theory, especially in Europe, and, a generation after he first brought the issue of different speech styles to the attention of sociologists and education planners, many of his insights remain relevant: 'Our society clearly values the elaborated codes. English-teaching in school concentrates on and rewards the elaborated, written language' (Fiske 2002: 72). That is the tyranny of writing in a different key and it makes us see language as an institution in a different light, though not as intended by Saussure. How the institution of language is employed to perpetuate social inequality was the overarching question in which Bernstein was interested. 'One code', he maintained, 'is not better than another . . . Society, however, may place different values on the orders of experience elicited through the different coding systems' (Bernstein 1971: 135). Clearly, in developed societies much value is placed on commanding a wide range of codes, including, especially, highly elaborated codes.

Another difference between elaborated and restricted codes is connected with dialectal variation. What has been variously called 'prestige language', 'standard language', etc., is in public parlance contrasted with regional dialects. While linguists are content to identify such a variety as one dialect among others – a 'literary dialect', for instance – normal language users tend to view the cultivated variety of written language as stripped of dialectal and locally specific features and hence more genuine. Since the elaborated code is closer to written language than restricted codes and exhibits fewer regional features, the perceived relationship between the two is that of a hierarchy of prestige. This is what ultimately gives rise to the social differentiation of language codes and thus to the basic idea that meaningful ways can be found of mapping linguistic variation not just onto geographic distance and temporal duration, but onto social conditions, too. The social conditions in question were, and to some extent still are, those of the industrialized countries where social class continues to be an important, if rather contentious, concept for social analysis. In Bernstein's words: 'Changes in the form of certain social relations, it is argued, act upon the principles that control selection of both syntactic and lexical options . . . Different forms of social relations can generate quite different speech-systems or linguistic codes by affecting the planning procedures' (Bernstein 1966: 254). This way of thinking has inspired research that led to the emergence of sociolinguistics as a scholarly discipline that in Europe, as well as in the US at the outset, was closely linked to the notion of compensatory education and equal opportunities for children of all social classes. For

> It has often been noted that working-class children do not perform so
> well educationally as might be expected, and it has been suggested
> that language may play an important role in this under-achievement.
> One component of this language problem is widely felt to be
> connected with dialect. Standard English is the dialect of education: it
> is spoken by most teachers; it is the dialect normally employed in
> writing; and it is rewarded in examinations. (Trudgill 1979: 15)

In this quotation all the ingredients of the sociolinguistic enterprise in its early state were present: educational achievement, social class, dialect and writing. A certain variety, Standard English, in the English-speaking world, is generally considered appropriate for writing, and those who have no or only poor command of this variety are denied many jobs and opportunities for social advancement. If only for this reason, the spectrum of varieties to be explored in sociolinguistics included, as a matter of course, explicit reference to writing. Bernstein and his early associates (e.g. Lawton 1968; Rosen 1972) saw language as a regulative system that, from the point of view of transmitting social structure and perpetuating stratification, was to be investigated by way of seeking an answer to the bigger question of how society is possible. As social systems change and adapt, this question must be reviewed periodically. Nowadays it would seem to lead straight to language, both spoken and written, since more social relations and institutions than ever before depend on and are mediated by written language. Yet, there is no theoretical framework which integrates the social aspects of writing. Bernstein's distinction of codes is important, but it never clarified the relationship between restricted and elaborated codes, on the one hand, and that between speech and writing, on the other. His central idea was that language, in all its complexity, is shaped by social relations serving the functions of community solidarity *and* social advancement, which cannot always be reconciled with each other.

Written language is the vehicle of education for speakers from various regions and tends to be conceived as the prototype of language from which spoken dialects are disorderly deviations on a lesser level. From an educator's point of view, Olson has reasoned that writing, by virtue of its physical constancy, is not just imbued with prestige, but also provides a model that allows us 'to see our language, our world and our minds in a new way' (Olson 1994: 258). Bernstein's notion that different learning patterns are associated with elaborated and restricted codes has a counterpart in Olson's emphasis on the different quality of cognitive orientation brought about by writing. Both perspectives rest on the insight that writing expands human communication capacity with implications that go far beyond the manifest difference in media between the audible and the visible.

The most general implication is that literate societies and individuals have a greater range of codes to choose from; and choose they must. Every communicative act requires a number of decisions to make it suitable to the purpose at hand, including the choice of medium and code. On a macro level, the society makes choices which have a formative bearing on the choices made by individuals as they grow into that society. It is with these choices, in as much as they concern writing, and the underlying determining factors that this book is concerned. It is intended to contribute to clarifying the social significance of writing and its complex relationships with social structure, linguistic varieties (codes), norms, attitudes, education and institutions that are predicated on written language. In the spirit of New Literacy Studies (Gee 1990), the ability to read and write is seen as interacting with social structure and cultural practices in addition to as a technical skill. It is the material and technical aspect of literacy that, at the present time, as when literacy was more widely disseminated by the printing press, once again reshapes society's communication patterns. Writing produces changes in language *and* society – in both cases by, among other things, making historical depth visible and thus bringing it to public attention. This is the subject of the next chapter.

DEFINITIONS

The following terminological clarifications prepare the ground for the chapters that follow.

Writing system. The term *writing system* as used in this book refers to an abstract type of graphic system. There are only a few such systems, distinguished by their basic operational units: word writing systems, syllabic writing systems, and phonetic writing systems. A secondary meaning of the term refers to the specific rules according to which the units of the system are interpreted in a given language. In the latter sense there are hence many writing systems, in the former only very few.

Orthography. Often used interchangeably with *spelling*, the term *orthography* means a standardized variety of a language-specific writing system; literally: Greek *orthos* 'correct' and *graphein* 'to write'. Spelling, unlike orthography, can be deviant, that is, irregular or unusual.

Script. The graphic form of a writing system is a *script*. The writing system employed in China and Hong Kong and Taiwan is the same, but two different scripts are employed, abbreviated characters in China and traditional characters in Hong Kong and Taiwan.

Written language. A written language is one that is used in writing for the purposes of non-immediate communication by its speech community. To be sure, this is a matter of degree; however, the definition excludes languages that have been reduced to writing by linguists without being put to use in written communication by their speakers.

Literacy. The ability to read and write. This ability defies objective definition, since the requirements for a person to be considered literate depend on historical and social circumstances. The term *functional literacy* is intended to cover this variability. In recent decades, the meaning of the word *literacy* has been extended to the ability to deal with various fields of knowledge, such as 'art literacy' or 'political literacy'. In this book such a usage is eschewed.

Social structure. This term characterizes the organization of society, referring to a relatively stable arrangement of institutions that regulate how various groups of people, distinguished by social class, gender, ethnicity, age, religion and language, live together.

QUESTIONS FOR DISCUSSION

1 In what sense did Saussure speak of the 'tyranny of writing' and in what other sense is the term used in this chapter? Is there any relationship between the two senses?

2 What do linguists need the IPA for, and how does it relate to language?

3 Consider some of the reasons why sociolinguistics has mostly ignored writing, and discuss the merits of the reasons for doing so.

2 The past in the present and the seeds of the public sphere

Writing is not a neutral and autonomous medium. (Thomas 1992: 74)

WRITING IN THE MARKETPLACE

The agora was the stage upon which communal life in the ancient Greek city-states unfolded, the epitome of a public place where people from all walks of life met in pursuit of their daily affairs. Primarily devoted to commercial transactions, the market place was also used at times for religious celebrations, rituals of various sorts, exercising justice, and political rallying or casting votes. There were both casual encounters and organized gatherings in the market place, which was associated with typical forms of communication, such as bargaining, haggling over prices, exchanging information, gossiping or discussing current events, but also making public announcements. The agora tended to be noisy, populated as it was by vendors, fishmongers, vintners, cloth merchants and shoemakers offering their merchandise and services while the town criers were stalking up and down the square. Medics and charlatans gave advice and philosophers attracted an audience by offering their views on the meaning of life. The magistrate convened hearings on the market place; the crowd that gathered there was an audience, rather than a readership. Yet, much of what we know about the ebb and flow of the exchange of goods, people and ideas on the Athenian agora has come down to us in the form of a large number of inscriptions painted or scratched on various everyday objects (Harris 1989). For writing, too, was becoming part of the 'media mix' of the ancient market place. These early expressions of popular Greek literacy go back to the eighth century BCE. In subject they range from indicating ownership of an object and debt ledgers to potsherds (*ostraca*) that citizens used as voting ballots to send one of their own into exile, as well as more complex texts such as public and private curses (Figure 2.1). Taken together they hold many insights into life in the Greek city-state, where writing was beginning

Figure 2.1 Bottom-up item of linguistic landscape: ostracon bearing the name of Perikles Xanthippos

to be increasingly important (Harvey 1966; Burns 1981; Havelock 1982; Thomas 1992).

Similar evidence of writing in public places came to light in the excavation of Pompeii in the eighteenth century. On the walls of the city that was buried under the ashes of Mount Vesuvius since 79 CE, a mixture of personal messages and political statements bear witness to Roman civilization. Insults and invectives were found side by side with official communications, sentences of the tribunal and announcements of public decisions. An advert announces: *M. Cerrinium aed pomari rog*, 'the fruit vendors recommend M. Cerrinius for aedile'. An aedile, commonly abbreviated *aed*, was a public office. *Rog*, too, is an abbreviated form of *rogatus*, whence 'rogatory', recognizable even to the English reader. About 3,000 electoral messages were written on walls of houses and other accessible surfaces of the city, which evidently functioned as a public space for, among other messages, political statements (Davis 1912–13: Vol. I).

Many of the inscriptions from the Athenian agora, Pompeii and other places throughout the ancient world are not so easily understood, but they can be *read*. Greeks and Italians today see that these texts are written with their alphabet in their language. They realize at a glance that, even if they fail to understand the message, they can relate to it, because it is their heritage that is on display, their own language, a bit distorted maybe, but recognizably Greek or Latin: 'From the oldest literary attestation of Ancient Greek to written and spoken Modern Greek many traits of the Greek language have survived more or less unchanged' (Gerö and Ruge 2008: 105). The continuity of the Greek language since antiquity is an important part of Greek self-understanding, comparable perhaps only with that of the Chinese. Both nations take pride in a long unbroken linguistic history which connects them to the most glorious moments of their past.

Without the written word, this would be quite impossible. Without the written word, we can take it for granted that our ancestors spoke, more or less, like we do; but we have no evidence to that effect, and even less evidence that they spoke differently. The difference is as important as the sameness; for it is on the basis of weighing similarities and distinctions that we define our own position relative to others. I do not intend to repeat or review here the literacy vs orality debate about the 'great divide' theory that attributes an autonomous force to the technology of writing that by and of itself brings about changes in virtually all spheres of social life (see, e.g., Barton and Papen 2010; Carlson, Fagan and Khaneko-Friesen 2010; Olson and Torrance 1991; Coulmas 1996: 305). Thomas' meticulous work on the interaction and overlap of literacy and orality in Classical Greece may better assist our understanding of what the introduction of writing into a society and culture implies. Her account represents a measured approach that acknowledges the gradual functional differentiation of oral and written communication and the embeddedness of literacy in oral tradition. While archaic Greek culture was not dominated by books, Thomas emphasizes the impact of public writing 'lending monumental weight to the new political organization of the developing city states' (1992: 72), particularly Athenian democracy.

HISTORICAL DEPTH

Before we return to the importance of public writing below, let us consider as another aspect of early literacy the historical horizon that writing opens up. This is of particular importance for languages such as Greek and Chinese. Inscriptions from antiquity attest many other languages, some older than the two just mentioned. What distinguishes Chinese and Greek from, for instance, Sumerian, Babylonian, Gothic and Etruscan is that these languages are no longer spoken, whereas Greek and Chinese survive. For everyone except academic historians and philologists the significance of languages whose tradition has been discontinued is limited to the past. Although Egyptian literary history is remarkably long, extending over some 3,000 years (Posener 1956), for the non-specialist it collapses in its entirety to a point in the distant past with no connection to our present-day life. By contrast, texts in Attic, Koine, Hellenistic and Byzantine Greek are linked in an unbroken line to the language of today, which thus has a retraceable time depth that goes far beyond speakers' capacity to remember. The impact on linguistic awareness of language time depth emerges only gradually, as notions of the authentic, the old and venerable, and the correct take shape. It is hardly a matter of course that written language should exercise an influence on spoken language, but history teaches that it did and continues to do so. All languages change and develop in the course of time, but only written languages carry the records of their own past with them, records that can be inspected, referred to as examples, idealized, quoted literally, falsified, canonized, condemned as 'tyranny', and translated.

Writing in the market place is quintessentially public. It changes the physical environment, adding to it a visual dimension of communication that brings in its wake new forms of interaction and awareness. Thus emerges a linguistic landscape – more properly perhaps, a cityscape – where language is not just heard, but also seen, permitting the spectator to contemplate and review the messages others have left behind, a moment or a decade ago, as the case may be. With the history of the inscribed object and the inscription, linguistic history, too, becomes part of the scenery. 'Linguistic landscape' is a relatively new term designating a new field of study (Landry and Bourhis 1997; Backhaus 2007; Shohamy and Grorter 2009), but writing had already changed the face of cities in antiquity. In the following sections of this chapter we will turn our gaze to some monuments that displayed writing openly. We find in them the seeds of the public sphere.

For all we know, writing was communicative rather than private from its inception (Harris 1986; Coulmas 2003), and some of its earliest functions are bound to public display. Property marks, brands and border stones, for example, speak to all members of a relevant community. Monumental inscriptions, too, appear early in all literate cultures. Ancient civilizations were not (fully) literate in the modern sense of the word, because in antiquity the art of writing was confined to scholarly elites rather than being a basic qualification for full participation in society (Goody 1987). Yet, even when writing was a specialized skill and literacy was restricted, the exhibition of visible language marked a fundamental change in the human habitat. It changed the way people saw the world, it changed their worldview, it changed their attitude towards and awareness of language, and in many ways it changed the organization of society.

The origin of writing coincided with urbanization, that is, the emergence of complex forms of social organization in cities and economic activity that produces a surplus beyond subsistence (Falkenstein 1954). That was not coincidental; rather, the one stimulated the other. Thus, it is on cities that linguistic landscape research must be focussed. Let us review then some prominent examples of linguistic landscaping in former times.

ELEMENTS OF THE LINGUISTIC LANDSCAPE

What are the elements of the linguistic landscape? Various answers have been proposed. Landry and Bourhis (1997: 25) identify 'public road signs, advertising billboards, street names, place names, commercial shop signs, and public signs on government buildings' as the elements that form the linguistic landscape. Cenoz and Gorter (2006: 71) take as their unit of analysis any establishment that displays language signs, while Backhaus (2007: 56) focusses on 'any piece of written text within a definable frame'. All of these methodological decisions are selective and well founded. The study of the historical linguistic landscape cannot be so selective, since it must make do with what is left, that is, inscriptions that have survived from the past. But the most general assumption that provides the rationale for linguistic landscape research also holds for historical settings: language displayed in the environment is not arbitrary or random (Shohamy and Gorter 2009: 2). Examining inscriptions with regard to the following three questions can therefore be expected to yield interesting insights about written language in society. Who produced them? Where were they placed? What were their functions?

THE CODEX HAMMURABI

One of the treasures of the Louvre in Paris is a stela[1] of black dorite that is some 3,700 years old. It is inscribed with the Codex Hammurabi in the Old Babylonian language in cuneiform script (Figure 2.2). Hammurabi, the king in whose name it was issued about 1772 BCE, ruled from 1792 to 1750 BCE over the world's first metropolis, Babylon. The set of laws the Code encompasses is one of his most remarkable legacies. Though not the oldest codified law, the Codex Hammurabi is the earliest known example of an entire body of law made public by a ruler to his people.

Figure 2.2 Top-down item of linguistic landscape: Codex Hammurabi (*c.* 1772 BCE)

It was an outstanding part of Babylon's rich linguistic landscape. The shining black stone monument stands 8 feet tall, showing on its upper half an image of the king praying in front of Sharmash, the divine guarantor of the law. The lower part bears the inscription of the 282 articles of the law, chiselled into the stone in exquisitely clear writing.

Turning to our first question: who produced it? The Codex Hammurabi marks the high point rather than the beginning of a literate culture. It was composed and compiled on order of the king, written by scholars with a thorough knowledge of the litigious habitude and customs of the land, and cut in stone by highly skilled artisans. The masons were working in specialized fields, sculptors cutting the images, and scribes incising the text. The stone slab that can be viewed in the Louvre today is a polished piece of work, an artefact that testifies to a high degree of division of labour typical of city life. Only a co-ordinated group of professionals, each in charge of a specific step in the process from conceptual planning through design and redaction to physical realization, could have produced it.

Where was the stela placed? The monument was intended to be erected in public view. The Codex Hammurabi was not discovered in

Babylon, but in a Persian city to which conquerors of a later period had carried it. But it can be concluded from other examples of laws inscribed on stelae that were excavated in Mesopotamian cities that it was erected in a conspicuous place in front of the palace or temple in the city centre where people would pass and assemble in large numbers. Wherever the exact location, it was placed in public view to be seen and read by anyone who could read. How large a part of the citizenry of Babylon was able to read we do not know, but it must have been sufficiently large to make the exercise worthwhile.

What functions did the Codex Hammurabi serve? The Code is a state law that regulates in clear and definite terms many aspects of social life. Without going into the specific legal norms, it can be said that by writing the laws on stone they were made immutable and protected from arbitrary abuse. The stela functioned both as an exhortation to obey the law and as an assurance of justice that everyone could invoke. By being put on open display the law was separated both from the norm-giver and from the judge. The inscribed stone became the law, which was detached from justice and execution. The 'letter of the law' thus acquired an authority in its own right. The stela literally embodied the law and with it the possibility of and call for justice. As a centrepiece of the metropolitan linguistic landscape, the Code is an early example of the objectification of law, and thus a first step in creating a public sphere. In addition to establishing a standard for behaviour to be observed by all, it also provided one for the Babylonian language, exemplifying the close conceptual relationship between grammar and law.

Every piece of writing is polyfunctional, but often one function predominates. The most noteworthy function of the Codex Hammurabi stela is regulatory and directive, stipulating behavioural norms as well as the sanctions to enforce them. From other collections of laws from Mesopotamian cities, such as the codes of Ur-Nammu (*c.* 2050 BCE) and the codes of Lipit-Ishtar (*c.* 1890 BCE), we know that this function was associated with writing early on. What distinguishes the Codex Hammurabi is that it publicly displays the law in its entirety.

THE ROSETTA STONE

Another landmark of the linguistic landscape of antiquity is the Rosetta Stone, discovered by François Xavier Bouchard, an officer of Napoleon's Egyptian expedition corps, and successfully used in the decipherment of Egyptian hieroglyphs by François Champollion (Parkinson 1999), to his everlasting glory. Kept in the Egyptian Gallery of the British Museum, this most celebrated piece of ancient writing is a fragment of a large black stela inscribed with a priestly decree concerning the cult of King Ptolemy V Epiphanes, issued on 27 March 196 BCE. The city of Sais in the delta of the Nile is thought to be where the stela was originally placed. The place at the coast where it was found, called 'Rosetta' by Europeans, did not exist in Ptolemaic Egypt.

Who produced the Rosetta Stone? Like the Hammurabi stela, the Rosetta Stone was created by skilled artisans on the basis of texts and designs provided by highly educated specialists. Again, it is not known how large a section of the population was literate, but it is evident that writing in public places was overwhelmingly important in Egypt and had been so for two millennia at the time the Rosetta Stone was inscribed. Those who composed the text and incised it into the polished surface of the stone were highly regarded and wanted for nothing. They were the architects of what was the most splendid linguistic landscape of antiquity. In Egyptian cities, monumental inscriptions were every-where. Many of the pillars, mural reliefs and sculptures that have come down to us have lost nothing of their grandeur and visual beauty. Their inscriptions are as clear and awe-inspiring as they were two or three millennia ago.

Where was the Rosetta Stone erected? The text on the Stone provides the answer to this question. It states that it was to be placed in a temple 'beside the statue of the Dual King Ptolemy' worshipped there: 'The stela was positioned against a wall in the outer area of a temple' (Parkinson 1999: 28). The text was clearly legible, although it required the reader to step in front of it, the letters being quite small. The temple was the centre of social life and the seat of power of the king-pharaoh, where people high and low would constantly pass by.

What functions did the Rosetta Stone serve? A large number of ancient Egyptian records are connected with cult. Temple walls and pillars are covered with magnificent hieroglyphic inscriptions, as are tombs, statues and other edifices. Royal decrees commanding reverence were common. They were meant for eternity, stone being a virtually indestructible surface (Assmann 1991). These monumental inscrip-tions exhibit very little change in style over a period of more than two millennia from the time they first appeared until the Egyptian tradition was discontinued. The Rosetta Stone dates from the late period of Egyptian civilization, which was subject to contact with and intrusion from other mighty empires, notably the Achamenid Persians and Macedonian Greeks. It was created in times as unsettled as those in which it was unearthed by French soldiers.

The Ptolemaic dynasty was Macedonian. Alexandria, a cultural centre of the ancient world, was a multilingual Greek city attracting merchants, scholars and artists from around the Mediterranean. Greek was the official language of the court and government, while Egyptian was used in the temples, the strongholds of tradition. Easing the tensions between ruler and ruled was a challenge for the administration. The decade preceding the coronation of Ptolemy V was marked by unrest and rebellions motivated partly by resentment against Greek rule. The decree on the Rosetta Stone bears witness to these tensions. It describes Ptolemy V, then just thirteen years old, as restoring order and making Egypt perfect. This is in keeping with a traditional pattern of royal decrees, but a special feature was that it was given in two languages and three scripts: Egyptian rendered in the formal hieroglyphic on top and the cursive demotic underneath, and Greek in the alphabet that had been in use since the seventh century BCE. The inscription on the stela in hieroglyphic as well as demotic has raised a number of questions, since the latter is a cursive derivative of the former, but one effect is evident: Egyptian occupies twice as much space on the stela as Greek. What is more, the arrangement of hieroglyphic, demotic and Greek, from top to bottom, suggests a meaningful order. In a culture permeated by symbolic meaning through a script that speaks to the eye with its stylized pictorial clarity like no other, it would be careless not to recognize here an emblematic hierarchy and an expression of deference to the Egyptian traditional high culture. The life world of Ptolemaic Egypt was one in which individuals bore both a Greek and an Egyptian name and prayed to gods with Greek and Egyptian names, and where distinct literary and religious traditions interacted in multiple ways.

The Rosetta Stone embodies many of the intricacies of language contact, language choice and linguistic hierarchy that form the substance of linguistic landscape research. Why was it composed in three scripts? Quirke speaks of 'an intricate coalescence of three vital textual traditions' (Andrews and Quirke 1988: 10). Overlapping and competing cultural and linguistic spheres created the need to compose the decree three times in order to appeal to the relevant groups in their preferred scripts: 'the traditional audience of Egyptian monuments, the gods and priests; the Egyptian-speaking literate populace; and the Greek administration' (Parkinson 1999: 30). The inscription itself acknowledges as much, proclaiming that the decree should be inscribed 'on a stela of hard stone in the script of god's words, the script of documents, and the letters of the Aegeans'.

THE BEHISTUN INSCRIPTION

Many other bilingual inscriptions, and some in more than two languages, have been preserved since antiquity. The most colossal of all
is the trilingual rock inscription of Darius I the Great (522–486 BCE),
king of Persia. Unlike other inscriptions of the great literate cultures of
antiquity, this one is located far from any metropolis on a rock face
along the old caravan route that connected Babylon and Ecbatana, the
capital of the Media Empire (Hamadân in modern Iran). The Zagros
Mountains are an isolated range that rises suddenly from a wide plain;
at their foot a number of springs feed into a small pool used by travellers and military expeditions to water their animals. It was here that
Darius chose to immortalize himself with an inscription some 300 feet
above the base of the rock face, thus leaving behind one of the most
remarkable examples of linguistic landscaping.

The famous Behistun inscription recounts how Darius was invested
by Ahuramazda, the great god of the Persians, with the power to oust
the usurper Gaumâta and to rule over the empire. It records the king's
military victories over insurgents in three languages: Old Persian, the
written language most widely used in the realm; Babylonian, the august
language of old; and Elamite, the language used to administer the
Achaemenid Empire. At the time, these were the three languages that
counted in this part of the world. The message proclaiming the glory of
Darius thus had universal appeal, although, astonishingly, it cannot be
read from below and never could, the cuneiform signs being much too
small to be made out by the naked eye.

This raises the question of the addressee. Who was supposed to read
the story of Darius the Great? The huge inscription containing tens of
thousands of signs chiselled meticulously into the polished rock took
years to complete. It was begun while Darius was still fighting the insurgents, and the original design had to be modified as he added victory to
victory (520–519 BCE). When the monumental labour was done, the narrow ridge on which the artisans stood engraving the rock was cut away,
making it almost impossible to come close enough to the text to read it –
or change it. (In 1835, Sir Henry Rawlinson, a British officer charged with
training the Iranian army, risked his life to scale the cliff and copy the
Old Persian inscription, the lowest part of the monument, the other two
being out of his reach.) While the text cannot be read, the monument
can be clearly seen from down below because the three inscriptions
are illustrated by huge bas-relief figures to impress the many travellers
passing by. The relief shows a winged picture of Ahuramazda floating
above a group of men: King Darius, his servants, and representatives of

subjugated peoples standing in front of him in fetters. By making the inscription inaccessible, Darius made sure that his claim to greatness before mortals and gods would be preserved forever and could not be tampered with. The three languages of the inscription testify not so much to a multilingual community life as to the all-inclusive appeal of its message and the vastness of the lands Darius had brought under his control. Meant as they were for eternity, the inscriptions of Behistun long outlasted the peoples who could read them and their gods, but continue to speak of them even today.

In the literate ancient world, bilingualism was not uncommon. In the Roman Empire it was pervasive, as illustrated by Donati (2002). Ultimately, inscriptions were meant to be read, and it was the target audience that determined whether an inscription was composed in one, two or several languages. Indian epigraphy too is replete with multilingual inscriptions (Salomon 1998). And in the Sino-centric world, monumental inscriptions in Chinese, Manchu, Mongolian, Tibetan and other languages are found in many places, such as the multilingual arch at the Juyongguan gate of the Great Wall (Waldron 1990). However, multilingualism is only rarely a topic explicitly addressed in these inscriptions. For this, the Rosetta Stone is the prime example. Public recognition of domain-specific linguistic diversity is thus what most distinguishes it.

MENETEKEL

As we have seen, establishing authority and law, securing respect for cult and symbolically acknowledging relevant groups and the order of society were important functions of written signs in the linguistic landscape of antiquity. They all testify to the effectiveness of writing as an instrument of control. The power-supportive function of writing is most conspicuous because these texts were hewn in stone in prominent places with much effort and diligence. They catch the eye as the legacy of high cultures of gods and priests and kings. However, evidence of the lowlier reaches of culture that coexisted with them, if less dazzling, has also been preserved in written records. The subversive potential of writing to undermine authority was recognized as soon as literacy had caught on as a learnable skill. Graffiti, the writing on the wall, is its most eloquent testimony. By whom, where, to what end? With regard to our three questions, graffiti is distinctly different from other elements of the linguistic landscape.

The proverbial 'writing on the wall' refers to the Biblical story of King Belshazzar of Babylon, who, on the occasion of an extravagant feast, was confronted with mysterious writing on the wall of the palace: 'Mene-tekel-parsin', an Aramaic phrase interpreted by a sage as a warning that the king's days were numbered and his empire would break up (Daniel 5,25). A text by an unknown author scratched, etched, incised, and nowadays sprayed, on a wall, which challenges authority – that is the essence of graffiti. A message that would perhaps be dangerous or embarrassing to express in the company of others is left as a trace for all to see, a warning, a call to arms, an exaltation, a slur. Graffiti speaks to us of subculture, resistance, sacrilege and profanity, contributing its share to establishing a public sphere.

All of the applications we associate with it today were present in antiquity: humour, slander, obscenity, lust, political passion, disclo-sure, accusation. The excavation of Pompeii, for example, has brought to light a wealth of wall writing, ranging from the rather modern-sounding *pecunia non olet* 'money doesn't stink' and *lucrum gaudium* 'profit is happi-ness', through bragging about sexual prowess, praise and insults, to the election advertisements mentioned above (Wallace 2005). Yet another function of graffiti is as a statement of the author's existence, which seems to satisfy a universal impulse. A famous example is the graffiti scratched by Greek mercenaries on the left leg of the colossal statue of Ramses II (1278–1213 BCE) at the façade of the Great Temple of Ramses at Abu Simbel, Egypt. It was written many centuries after Ramses' death, but the exact date and author of the inscription are a matter of specu-lation, as is typical of graffiti writers who want to get their message out without being held responsible for it. The same potential that writing offers to kings determined to immortalize their heroic deeds in grand inscriptions is available to tramps with nothing to announce but that they 'were here'. The chances that readers of such graffiti would know the author, and respond and engage in a meaningful exchange, are remote, but that does not seem to be the purpose. Rather, associating oneself with something great by leaving a trace and inscribing one-self into history is a more likely motivation of these vacuous messages addressed to strangers.

THE TAJ MAHAL

Remembering, honouring and committing to eternity people and events is a capacity writing shares with images, which, like letters, characters and hieroglyphs, appeal to the eye and our sense of beauty. Calligraphy is a potential of writing that flows out of its visual real-ization, put into practice to a greater or lesser extent in any literate culture. Its exceptionally high level of development in Arabic literacy is a response to the image prohibition of Islam. The 'holy scrip(ture)' is to be understood literally. Every Arabic letter is divine. Countless buildings throughout the Islamic world are adorned with calligraphic inscriptions, homage to God and the art of writing. One of the most stupendous examples is the Taj Mahal, built 1633–53 in memory of Arjumand Bano Begum, wife of Shah Jahan, as a tribute to love the world would never forget. The most skilled architects, inlay craftsmen, masons and calligraphers created this incomparable mausoleum overlooking the Yamuna River in the city of Agra.

The inscriptions were selected and composed to form an epitaphic programme by calligrapher Amanat Khan on order of Shah Jahan. Interlaced with vining floral designs, they cover large parts of the walls, arches and friezes of the building. Where the inscriptions are placed in elevated places and in arches the letters are deliberately distorted to correct the perceived distortion from the beholder's point of view. Most of the texts are Qur'anic surahs, including entire chapters that are read out as part of the Islamic funeral ceremony. The writing is in black lettering in the Thuluth script in a style brought to its highest refinement by Persian calligraphers. The inscriptions are a testimony of eternal love and the profoundest sense of loss as well as the consolation sought and found in Islam, exhibiting the humanity of Islam and its overwhelming importance in Mughal India. The texts could be read by the literate elite, and their beauty admired by those unversed in the art of writing. It has been suggested that the form and location of the building was meant to match the message of the texts and that the mausoleum is an allegorical representation of the Throne of Allah above the Garden of Paradise on the Day of Judgement.

Whether or not this interpretation is valid is none of our concern. It is mentioned here only to highlight the conceptual interaction between message, inscription and inscribed surface as an important aspect of linguistic landscaping. It is in the nature of calligraphy that it oscillates between the aesthetic and the informative. In the case of Islamic calligraphy the former often supersedes the latter (Blair 2008). The highly stylized inscriptions on such monuments as the seventh-century Dome of the Rock in Jerusalem, the eleventh-century Qut'b Minar in Delhi, or the seventeenth-century Masjid-I Shah in Isfahan are legible only to specialists with extensive knowledge of Classical Arabic. Their location above eye-level does not facilitate the task of reading them. The information contained in the inscription is not easily accessible. Yet these monuments are undeniably elements of the linguistic landscape, as are others where the discrepancy between 'what is in the text' and 'what speaks to the eye' is even more evident.

DISPLACEMENT

This is true especially of inscribed monuments that have been displaced, such as the Codex Hammurabi stela discussed above. As booty, souvenirs, folkloristic emblems and other eye-catching items, displaced monuments or replicas thereof are popular elements of linguistic landscaping. One conspicuous genre is that of obelisks. Originating in Pharaonic Egypt, these monuments found many admirers. Some of these massive monoliths had already been transported to other countries in antiquity (Curran *et al.* 2009). Today, thirteen of thirty original large obelisks form an integral part of the linguistic landscape of the eternal city, Rome (Figure 2.3). Some were brought there as plunder, for example the obelisk on the Piazza del Popolo, which Octavianus took home after he had conquered Egypt in 31 CE. Others were made to order, such as the one in Piazza Navona, which was made at Aswan to commemorate the accession of Emperor Domitianus in 81 CE. The durability of writing in stone is exemplified impressively by another displaced landmark, the obelisk placed on one of the most beautiful urban squares, the Place de la Concorde in the centre of Paris. Dating from Ramses II of the nineteenth Dynasty, 1304–1237 BCE, it was transported from Luxor to the French capital in the nineteenth century. No Parisian outside university departments of Egyptology and archaeology can read it, but its symbolic significance is great. As the result of a battle lost, not by the Egyptians, but by the French against the British, the Rosetta Stone that enabled the breakthrough in deciphering Egyptian hieroglyphs is kept in London.[2] It is, therefore, no trifle to remind the world that this ancient literary heritage was rescued from oblivion by the French.

Many obelisks and other inscribed monuments have travelled to become a de-contextualized and then re-contextualized element of a linguistic landscape far removed from their places of origin. Again, these grandiose examples illustrate a more general aspect of linguistic landscaping awaiting systematic study, that is, linguistic signs hailing from another place and another time. Because of the cultural, linguistic and temporal distance, the information content of many of these signs has receded into the background, giving way to a symbolic message. Yet, while they have been removed from the environment of their original readership, a universal meta-text remains: if you care to decipher it, a message is here, a message that is addressed to strangers, for a text

Figure 2.3 Egyptian obelisk dating from 595–589 BCE, brought to Rome in 10 BCE by Emperor Augustus; today in front of the Italian parliament building on Piazza di Montecitorio

displayed in the open is accessible to all (who can read); no one can be barred from participating in the open domain.

COMMUNICATION WITH STRANGERS

Various lessons can be drawn from the landmarks examined above. In antiquity, as today, linguistic signs openly displayed were meant to be read. In very general terms this means that linguistic landscape research must take issue with the questions of 'who is able to read this sign?' and 'who reads it?' Every inscription conveys a message about itself that refers to the language in which it is composed: 'There is someone out there who reads language x.' Next, the readership of any sign openly displayed is targeted by the writer, who may or may not be officially authorized to do so. Government decrees, commercial advertisements and spontaneous scribble vie for space, attention and influence. A useful distinction of communication flows in the linguistic landscape has been proposed by Ben-Rafael (2009: 49). A 'top-down' flow originates from public bodies authorized to diffuse information to common citizens, whereas a 'bottom-up' flow contains items produced by an indefinite mass of actors distinguished only by the ability to write.

Top-down items and bottom-up items constitute the elements of linguistic landscape as a cultural scene, formed by interested agents whose motivations and intentions pertaining to information content, language choice and symbolic significance, to the extent they can be inferred, must be reckoned with in the analysis. The frame conditions of this undertaking spring from social organization, networks, education and power relations, on one hand, and from the nature of writing and technology, including the writing surface – stone, paper, electronic screens, etc. – on the other. Much separates giant TV screens and running message displays powered by means of light-emitting diodes from stone stelae and rock inscriptions, but an essential function has stayed the same: landmarks of the city are to be read, which was and remains a defining feature of city life.

These landmarks, as well as other elements of the urban linguistic landscape, are addressed to and read by the public. Public communication potentially involves everyone. According to Neidhardt (1994: 10), it occurs whenever a communicator cannot control the boundaries of his or her audience. This criterion counterposes the private and the public sphere, the former being centred on the family where all members and other participants know one another, whereas communication in the public sphere is 'open to strangers' (Warner 2002: 74). It is worth noting here that 'openness to strangers' has been emphasized by social scientists as a defining feature of communication in the public sphere (Calhoun 2003; Warner 2002). While control over the boundaries of one's audience and control over access was clearly more rigid in antiquity than in modern times, the point to note is that the inclusion of strangers in communication is a structural corollary of writing. Speaking in the public and in the private spheres can be overheard by unintended listeners and eavesdropped upon only when and where it happens and never in the absence of the speaker. But once a message has been committed to writing it is separated from its originator and begins a life of its own. By virtue of the physical properties of the medium its originator, short of destroying the document, cannot contain its diffusion. That is the nature of mediated communication where messages are detached from their originators, and originators and recipients can remain strangers to one another for ever. The prototype of this kind of communication is writing, which must thus be understood as a structural precondition to the emergence of the public sphere.

As originally conceptualized in the 1960s by Habermas (1991), the public sphere is a connecting link between the personal environment of the family and the depersonalized state. In the bourgeois society he analyses, it involves a relatively stable arrangement of institutions that regulate how variously defined groups of people live together as a virtual or imaginary community 'made up of private people gathered together as a public and articulating the needs of society with the state' (Habermas 1991: 176). Of course, the early tokens of linguistic landscape discussed above do not count as expressions of the public sphere, which Habermas sees emerge only in the eighteenth century in the wake of more widespread literacy, a higher degree of individual autonomy, rule of law, a press and, generally, a higher quality of participation by members of society. It was the literate bourgeoisie that spearheaded the coming into existence of the public sphere at the threshold of modernity (Figure 2.4). The consumption and relatively free discussion of literary works was the fertile ground on which grew a new phenomenon, public opinion, which in Habermas' analysis was instrumental in differentiating state and society. Early precursors of public opinion and its articulation as a crucial element of the social order can be recognized in some of the elements of the linguistic landscape of the Athenian agora. Potsherds incised only with a name anonymously cast as ostraca were an instance of public choice on the basis of communication open to strangers. They are material testimony to active engagement in political life and social organization, which is not accepted unquestioningly and dictated by tradition but shaped by a community of active participants who share a public sphere 'as an on-going process of communication open to strangers [which] is also a form of and a process for forming solidarity and a sense of belonging' (Koller 2010: 265).[3]

Both the instrumental and the symbolic functions of writing constitute antecedent conditions for the social mechanisms that lead to the emergence of a public sphere. Only those able to scratch a name on a potsherd can participate in the ballot, and through its visual distinctiveness writing is a strong symbol of community, as the discussions regularly accompanying writing reforms remind us – a topic which will be discussed at length in Chapter 6. In the form of ostraca, writing is an instrument of political participation that permits individuals to develop a sense of autonomy and the ability to influence

Figure 2.4 In the public sphere: reading the newspaper. Honoré
Daumier, *Le Charivari*, 1847

their environment. It is precisely in this sense that Thomas' (1992: 72)
remark, quoted above, about the impact of writing on the political
organization of the Greek city state, must be understood.

Although writing was not the sole cause of the features just mentioned, it is hard to imagine their coming into existence without it, for
writing both individualizes and socializes. On one hand, it forces each
member of the citizen body to recognize the written word as appeal-
ing individually to him or her, and on the other, it creates a community of those to whom it appeals. At the same time, by dissociating
the word from its speaker, writing creates abstract authorship, that is,
authority, helping officialdom to constitute itself and consolidate its
power.

Writing is the origin of the public sphere in yet another sense. In
antiquity, both social and grammatological factors made literacy an

arena for specialists. On the one hand, lack of economic resources did not allow the freeing of a large segment of the population from labour in order to acquire schooling. And on the other hand, the complicated nature of early writing systems also stood in the way of mass literacy. Yet even under these circumstances, writing on open display holds the potential of its acquisition by the uninitiated. It is a genie let out of the bottle. In the long run it cannot be controlled, although it can take a long time for the masses to appropriate it. In the form of top-down and bottom-up items of the linguistic landscape, writing embodies the dialectics of power and resistance. A potent tool to secure institutional authority, it can also be turned against the powers-that-be and used to challenge authority. This double-edged nature of writing must not be misconstrued as evidence that, like other technologies, it is neutral and autonomous. It is not, for it is constitutive of a kind of public domain that does not exist under the conditions of exclusively oral communication. In oral society, communication with strangers is not really possible. In public speeches the audience may be unknown to the speaker, but he or she cannot remain anonymous, and in face-to-face encounters the first exchange of words establishes a relationship between the interlocutors. In contrast, writing-mediated communication allows writer and reader to remain unknown to each other for ever.

Communication with strangers is a defining feature of the public sphere and of linguistic landscape. The remains of the linguistic landscape of ancient cities, whose messages we read unbeknown to their originators, whom we will never know, remind us that it was through the mediation of writing that this kind of anonymous communication first became possible. Writing thus makes a difference, for both society and language. Those populating the linguistic landscape cannot but interact with it, positioning their own communication behaviour, recognizing change and heritage. Language in the linguistic landscape acquires perceptible historical depth, and society expands its communication practices. As a modern research domain, linguistic landscape is the study of writing on display in the public sphere. While the 'public sphere' does not necessarily refer to an identifiable space, it presupposes an urbanized society. By the same token, linguistic landscape research is typically focussed on *urban* environments. Linguistic landscape is really linguistic cityscape, especially in multilingual settings. All the pioneering studies are about cities: Brussels (Tulp 1978), Montreal (Landry and Bourhis 1997), Jerusalem (Spolsky and Cooper 1991), Paris and Dakar (Calvet 1990), among others.[4] Significantly, it was in cities that writing evolved and unfolded its full potential, because complex forms of coexistence and interaction require forms of expression and communication freed from the limitations that come with the volatility and directness of speech. Linguistic landscape is a viewpoint from which to study language in urbanized society, the object of investigation being the multidimensional distribution of languages and varieties in the city, as opposed to the regional distribution of varieties of language investigated in traditional dialectology. Like the public sphere, the linguistic landscape is not a neutral or immutable place, but an arena in which interested participants vie for influence, changing it in the process. As we will see in Chapter 7, the electronic media revolution has changed and continues to change the linguistic landscape and the public sphere. Written language is at the centre of this revolution. In the two chapters that follow, we will therefore take a closer look at what writing does to language and what literacy does to society.

QUESTIONS FOR DISCUSSION

1 In what sense does writing provide language with historical depth?
2 What can we learn from ostraca about language use and political participation in Greek city-states?
3 What do the categories 'top-down items' and 'bottom-up items' in the linguistic landscape mean? What is their significance for studying language in social settings? Discuss examples from your own environment.
4 How do the concepts of linguistic landscape and public sphere relate to each other?

3 Written and unwritten language

The transition of a language to written recording involves profound transformations, one of the most salient being the reduction of the fluctuation characteristic of the spoken word in favour of a congelation of the used registry. (Cardona 2009: 132)

LINGUISTIC RESOURCES

The majority of the languages of the world have never been written, but the vast majority of the world's population learn to read and write. This implies that virtually everywhere the division of communicative labour between the oral and written modes corresponds to specific sociolinguistic arrangements that assign different functions to different languages. One way of looking at these arrangements is by considering languages as resources. Two dimensions for systematizing linguistic resources are stipulated here: (1) the reference group, and (2) a language's functional potential. As regards the first dimension, the question is 'Whose resources?', whereas the second asks: 'What kind of resources?' The reference group is identified in terms of size and group-defining features, ranging in descending order from the all-encompassing to the minimal unit: world, nation state, ethnicity, organization, family and individual. The functional dimension is subdivided into various kinds of resources: intellectual, cultural, emotional – symbolic, social and economic. Using these two dimensions, a matrix can be set up as illustrated in Table 3.1.

Sumerian is extinct; however, being one of the earliest languages ever committed to writing it can be considered an intellectual and cultural resource of the world, much like a designated world heritage site, and perhaps also as a cultural resource for Iraq. There is, however, no nation or ethnicity for which Sumerian is an intellectual, emotional – symbolic, social or economic resource. Organizations such as scholarly societies and their individual members may consider Sumerian a resource, even in economic terms, as it provides the basis for the livelihood of some

Table 3.1 *A matrix for languages as resources*

Reference group \ Resources	Intellectual	Cultural	Emotional–symbolic	Social	Economic
World					
Nation					
Ethnicity					
Organization					
Family					
Individual					

On the basis of this matrix, languages can be compared from the point of view of what resources they represent for various reference groups. The cells of the matrix can be filled with pluses and minuses or more detailed information. Consider three examples in Tables 3.2, 3.3 and 3.4.

Table 3.2 *Sumerian as a resource*

Reference group \ Resources	Intellectual	Cultural	Emotional–symbolic	Social	Economic
World	+	+	−	−	−
Nation	−	+	−	−	−
Ethnicity	−	−	−	−	−
Organization	+	?	+	+	+
Family	−	−	−	−	−
Individual	+	+	+	+	+

Table 3.3 *French as a resource*

Reference group \ Resources	Intellectual	Cultural	Emotional–symbolic	Social	Economic
World	+	+	+	+	+
Nation	+	+	+	+	+
Ethnicity	+	+	+	+	+
Organization	+	+	+	+	+
Family	+	+	+	+	+
Individual	+	+	+	+	+

Table 3.4 *Occitan as a resource*

Reference group / Resources	Intellectual	Cultural	Emotional–symbolic	Social	Economic
World	–	–	–	–	–
Nation	–	?	–	–	–
Ethnicity	–	–	–	–	–
Organization	–	–	–	–	–
Family	–	+	+	+	–
Individual	–	+	+	+	–

academics. Its role as a cultural resource is, perhaps, debatable, and in what sense Sumerian could be a resource for families is hard to imagine.

The matrix for French looks different. French plays a certain role at the world level, for instance as one of the official languages of the UN and other international organizations. The language of a rich and vibrant literature, it can claim to be a cultural resource on every level. As an emotional–symbolic resource it is highly valued: at the national level, above all in France; by ethnic minorities such as the Québécois and the Walloons; and by organizations (e.g. Francophonie, an organization of polities and governments that use French traditionally), as well as at family and individual levels. The same holds for the social and economic resources that French embodies. Serving social networks at the global, national, minority and organizational levels, and by implication families and individuals, it is also a significant economic resource on all of these levels. Thus, all matrix cells for French are marked '+'.

Consider next the matrix for Occitan, spoken by elderly people in southern France. Its cells, with a few exceptions, are full of minuses. Pluses are allotted as a resource only at the family and individual level, where Occitan plays a certain role as a cultural and emotional good that also serves social network functions. However, most Occitan speakers do not consider themselves a separate ethnicity, and at the national and world level it does not constitute a significant resource, although as a documented part of France's linguistic history it might be considered a cultural resource at the national level.

To drive the exercise to the extreme, under what conditions would a matrix contain only minuses? In fact, these conditions obtain for many languages, namely those that have become extinct without leaving a trace. For instance, unlike Sumerian, the Kwadi language of Angola disappeared without any documentation. We know that it was spoken by a small community until a few decades ago, but not much else. The last speaker apparently died in the 1980s. What little information is available about Kwadi is not enough even to classify this language, let alone to continue studying it. It does not constitute a resource in the sense of the categories of the matrix for any of the reference groups.

Instead of pluses and minuses, we could fill the cells with relevant information to the effect, for example, that French is considered by the French and by others an important intellectual resource and is popular as a foreign language which happens to be the basis of a fairly large industry and hence constitutes an economic resource; that elites in several countries use French to create and sustain supranational networks; that Occitan and other languages of France do not serve as social, economic and intellectual resources, or not in the same way as French; and so on. It is common knowledge that different languages serve different functions in their respective environments. The binary matrix is just a convenient tool for highlighting and systematizing the more important distinctions. As it turns out, most of these distinctions have to do with whether or not or to what extent a language is used in writing. What is it that writing does to language? This question, again, calls for answers on two levels, the social and the linguistic.

SOCIAL CHARACTERISTICS OF WRITTEN AND UNWRITTEN LANGUAGE

As the example of Sumerian shows, a dead language can still be a resource, provided there are written records. For living languages, too, the literary status is a decisive factor. In many, though not all, Western societies one dominant all-purpose language is considered the unmarked case. It is the language that everyone speaks, that one is taught how to write at school, in which one's birth certificate is issued and one's tombstone is engraved; the language of the mass media, higher education, law and cult. Languages such as English, French, Italian, Spanish, Dutch and German in their proper national environments fill this bill. There are minorities with their own languages, to be sure, but that is a different matter. The point at issue here is that in the corresponding speech communities it is assumed that the hegemonic language covers the whole functional range, from the most informal and intimate to the most formal and official. French, German, Dutch, etc., can be used in colloquial chats at a bar counter as well as in petitions submitted to an authority. Different registers are used for these purposes, but both are understood as expressions of one and the same language. Obvious differences in 'diction' and 'style', rather than being ignored or regarded as deviations, are constructed as function-specific manifestations of one highly cultivated language. The underlying notion of the unity of spoken and written language is strongly ideological, reflecting as it does the maxim 'write as you speak', which has informed mother tongue education in Europe since the early modern period. This principle, however, never meant that everybody should write as he or she speaks and that, therefore, the variability of speech should be mirrored in writing.

Both the all-purpose language and the 'write as you speak' principle are ideal types, models for, rather than faithful portrayals of, linguistic practices. In fact, if for the purpose of this chapter we ignore most recent developments in electronic communication, the linguistic ecologies of most speech communities contain rather clear ideas about how language resources are to be employed, including what is and what is not suitable for writing. 'Write as you speak' was never meant for, or applied to, all speakers and all speech forms. As a result the language behaviour of the reference groups presented in Table 3.1 is based on a hierarchy of languages or codes or varieties.

The latter two terms are sometimes helpful in steering clear of the terminological pitfalls in this terrain. One such pitfall is the well-known difficulty of determining what constitutes a language. Linguists have not been able to solve it satisfactorily, admitting that purely linguistic criteria are insufficient to explain how continua of speech forms are divided into languages. For describing the distribution of language variation and language varieties is influenced by sociocultural ideologies operating within a society (Wolfram 1997; Coulmas 2005: 21f.). For instance, on the basis of structural and lexical comparisons of Dutch and Swiss German with Standard German it would be well nigh impossible to predict that the former but not the latter is considered a language. Historical and political factors must be resorted to if we want to understand the difference between the two and their relation to German, including, of course, the fact that Dutch is used in writing, whereas Swiss German – more accurately, the Swiss German dialects – typically is not. However, as discussed in Chapter 1, writing must not interfere with linguistic description, and accordingly differences arising from literary status and other language-external factors are ignored. For structural linguistic purposes this is a defensible position, but sociolinguists cannot follow this lead without losing sight of the most important social distinctions in the linguistic ecology. German has a telling term that is relevant in this connection: *Mundart*, literally 'mouth-manner' or 'manner of speaking'. Swiss German dialects are *Mundarten*. Their distinctly oral nature is acknowledged by the Swiss, who refer to German as

Schriftdeutsch, 'written German', a term not commonly used in German German. In their everyday terminology, the Swiss Germans thus identify their written language as German. In contrast, in the Netherlands, writing marks the departure of Dutch from German. Dialects spoken in northern Germany and in the eastern parts of the Netherlands border are quite close, but compulsory education has turned their speakers into Dutch speakers on one side of the border, and German speakers on the other.

The French term corresponding to *Mundart* is *patois*. In Old French 'patois' meant 'vulgar language, incomprehensible speech of the illiterate classes'. Nowadays 'patois' is defined as 'the local dialect of a region, used usually in informal everyday situations, as opposed to the language used in literature, education, etc.'[1] There are not many illiterates in France any more, but the association of patois with orality persists. It is an unlettered variety. In France, both vernacular varieties of French and other speech forms that bear no close relationship to French may be classified as patois. Since, like dialect, this term has decidedly derogatory overtones, it is not generally used in sociolinguistics (except as a term for varieties of Caribbean English). Not only that – since, in many societies, vernacular dialects are perceived as not just rustic but deficient linguistic systems, sociolinguists have endeavoured to correct this perception. Much like Bernstein (1966) argued that a restricted code in and of itself should not be regarded as inferior, and Labov (1969) made the case for recognizing the internal logic of Black English Vernacular rather than dismissing it as slang, French sociolinguists dealt with patois. Since, like race, gender and age, vernacular speech is a social marker that gives rise to discrimination, demonstrating the rule-governed nature of these varieties has always been more than just a grammatical exercise. Establishing the dignity of non-hegemonic speech forms was the real purpose.

In this connection, Calvet (1987) speaks of 'language wars', criticizing the systematic suppression of substandard speech forms by the centralized French state. In his view, Occitan is a language on a par with French, since on the grounds of internal linguistic characteristics – phonology, morphology and syntax – the latter has nothing that elevates it above the former. However, the status of a language in a society is not determined on the basis of structural features alone, if at all. The fact that a speaker thinks she speaks patois rather than Occitan is indicative to Calvet only of her distorted linguistic self-awareness and the low status of Occitan. Marfany (2010) takes issue with this point of view, criticizing it as misguided. Speakers' linguistic self-awareness is an important element of any sociolinguistic arrangement, no matter how it has come into being and whether and to what extent it reflects linguistic facts. Linguists, Marfany argues, are justified in dismissing ideological notions such as *patois*, but sociolinguists are ill advised to do so, for languages, 'real languages, those which exist or have existed in the real world, are not givens, but historical constructs, the product of more or less protracted historical processes, that is to say, processes of a social and not a linguistic nature' (Marfany 2010: 6).

As for Occitan, an ideological battle has been fought off and on between the French Ministry of Education, with its basically monolingual agenda and restrictive policy on minority languages, on one side, and, on the other, activists who see themselves engaged in a national liberation struggle calling for the recognition of their language as being on a par with French, Spanish, Italian, etc., insisting that there is an Occitan nation (EBLUL-France 2007). Under these circumstances, which are typical for public discourse about minority languages today, it is hard to imagine how the question of 'language or patois' could be decided objectively, that is, without ideological bias. Marfany (2010: 7) argues that at issue here are social, not linguistic, realities. Thanks to 'primarily social homogenization of pre-existing vernaculars', French is rightly considered a language, whereas Occitan and other Romance vernaculars, such as Venetian, which 'toward the end of the Middle Ages, came close to becoming a language, but never did', are not. In the days of the Venetian Republic, its language enjoyed considerable prestige, but it was eclipsed by the rise of the dialect of Tuscany as Italy's national language. Today Venetian is considered, by its own speakers and others, an Italian dialect limited to informal contexts, although on genetic grounds its classification as a sister language of Italian would be more accurate (Ferguson 2007). Artico (1976), a speaker of Venetian, refers to it, notably, as a 'dialect'.

Patois, *Mundart* and *dialect* in the non-technical sense are social rather than linguistic facts that, within a relevant regional or national context, form part of a status hierarchy with a hegemonic language at the top. The variability of dialects and their relative closeness or distance in a given sociolinguistic setting are a challenge for linguistic analysis, but mean little when it comes to understanding coexisting speech forms, some but not all of which are recognized by their speakers and others as languages. When speakers refer to certain varieties in a derogatory manner as patois and qualify their own speech as patois, they describe the existing hierarchy as they see it. In so doing they may give expression to, and thus perpetuate, the hegemonic linguistic ideology which, however, is part of what the sociolinguistic arrangement is all about. The fact that in France both substandard varieties of French and unrelated languages are called 'patois' only underscores this point. 'Patois' and 'language' differ not so much on linguistic grounds as in terms of position in a status hierarchy. At times, these sociolinguistic arrangements and the language ideologies supporting them are challenged by disempowered or marginal groups, sometimes successfully. As will be discussed in more depth in Chapter 6, writing invariably plays a central role in any design for changing a status hierarchy and laying claim to language status for a variety that has none. Having a written norm is an indispensable, though not a sufficient, condition for striving for higher status. A *patois* or *Mundart*, as understood by its speakers, does not usually enter the competition, for, as an informant quoted by Marfany (2010: 9) put it, 'il ne s'écrit pas' – it is not written. From a sociohistorical point of view it does not matter much whether a variety for which status as a language is sought is (e.g. Occitan) or is not (e.g. Breton) closely related to the hegemonic language (e.g. French) of the hierarchy of which it is a part. More important are social power differentials defining the relationships among their speakers. For, typically, it is not that a prestigious language with its potential of resources secures its speakers a dominant position in society, but, on the contrary, that prestige accrues to a language as its speakers gain a dominant position relative to others. This causality is sometimes obscured by the fact that a language retains its preeminent position in a status hierarchy longer than its original speakers in the society.

Any sociolinguistic arrangement encompasses written and unwritten speech forms which, taken together, in a function-specific division of labour, constitute the totality of the community's linguistic resources and combine to satisfy its communication needs. From a sociolinguistic point of view, it goes without saying that such a division of labour does not concern language as a natural faculty, but language as a sociohistorical construct, a written norm being the load-bearing pillar of the dominant language's hegemonic position. Contrary to the notion that all languages are equal, cherished by linguists, speech varieties that coexist in a common sociolinguistic arrangement are unequal. In most cases, this is not contested by, or a matter of acrimony on the part of, speakers of subordinate dialects, patois, etc. According equal status to all speech varieties is not practical or desirable, but the linguistic tenet discussed in Chapter 1 – that writing is unimportant – obscures this fact. Marfany, not being a linguist, makes a case for correcting this:

> Without bringing the written language into the picture, we are bound to get wrong both the sociology and the history of any language. For one thing, *without writing there is no language* [emphasis added] . . . And

in fact, the fundamental difference between a dialect and a patois can be expressed in the following terms: a dialect does not have a written form because it does not *need* one – its written form is the (written) language. The Cockney speaks Cockney (i.e., dialectal English), but writes in (standard) English. A patois does not have a written form because it *cannot have* one. Its speakers do not write it because it cannot and must not be written. (Marfany 2010: 9)

Marfany's outspoken position – no writing, no language – is a clear and articulate counterpoint to Bloomfield's statement, quoted in Chapter 1, that 'in order to study writing, we must know something about language, but the reverse is not true' (Bloomfield 1933: 21). Both could not be right – or could they? In fact, upon closer consideration, their views turn out to be less irreconcilable than would initially appear, for their disciplinary points of view and fields of interest are quite diverse. Bloomfield, an American linguist, was confronted with speech forms used by many communities all over the North American continent that had no written form, but that, in terms of structural diversity, intercommunicability and sociolinguistic arrangements, could not reasonably be called dialects of each other or any written language. He therefore downplayed the importance of writing, calling it a handicap for linguistic analysis. In contrast, Marfany is a Catalan historian whose principal interest is in the social and cultural history of European nations and nationalism, especially in the sphere of Romance languages. Here, the importance he assigns to writing is cogent, and the folk categories of patois and dialect have analytic value, reflecting as they do the social attitudes underpinning the sociolinguistic arrangements he is concerned with. Only speech varieties that have a written form can lay claim to language status. When we confine our examination to the sphere of Romance languages, obtaining this status, rather than depending on structural features, is a matter of historical contingencies and political decisions. Consider, for instance, Picard, which enjoys language status in francophone Belgium, but not in France, where it is regarded as a French dialect. The principal (written) Romance languages are Spanish, Portuguese, French, Italian, Romanian and Catalan. In addition dozens of varieties are used orally, mainly in informal settings. Taken together they form the Romance dialect continuum, which, with the exception of Eastern Romance (Romanian), is geographically contiguous and does not offer easy inherent classification. In terms of the intellectual, cultural, emotional–symbolic, social and economic resources they embody, the said (written) languages surpass the rest. However, 'surpass' is not really the right word, for, in most cases, what is at issue is not a matter of comparison or competition. Rather, the normal division of linguistic labour for virtually all speakers of Romance varieties without language status is not 'write as you speak', but 'write the (national, written, literary, standard) language and speak another (dialect, patois or minority language)'. In their understanding, as in many other parts of the world, writing is not, as Bloomfield (1933:21) put it, 'merely a way of recording language by means of visible marks', but what makes a language, as distinct from a 'mouth-manner'.

LINGUISTIC CHARACTERISTICS OF WRITTEN AND UNWRITTEN LANGUAGES

So far in this chapter differences between spoken language and written language have been explored from the point of view of functional division of labour in terms of resources and status. In this section we examine the question of whether there are any linguistic differences between written and unwritten language, and, if so, what they are. This question can be addressed in two distinct ways. One is by comparing oral and written language manifestations in the context of one and the same language: What are the structural differences between spoken French, English, Chinese, and written French, etc.? The other is by comparing a language with a long literary tradition with one that is used in oral communication only.

Since a grammar – etymologically from Greek *grammatike tekhne* 'the art of letters' – in the usual, non-technical sense of the word, is a set of rules that describe or prescribe how the written language works, the first question can be rephrased as follows: 'Is there a separate grammar of speech?' Inspired partly by the sociolinguistic project of studying substandard speech forms, a great deal of research about how best to analyse speech and what descriptive categories to use has accumulated (Roberts and Street 1997). The initial answer this research has produced is, yes, the grammar of oral language – such as Black English Vernacular, restricted code, youth jargon, informal conversation, etc. – is different, but a grammar it is. We just have to uncover the underlying principles, which differ to a large extent from the grammar of written language as a result of the different medial channels involved. There is no prosody in writing, for example, and no page we can turn back in speech. Participants in ordinary conversation are physically co-present, seeing each other. Why they speak, what they say and how they understand it depend on their visual participation. In contrast, communicating without reliance on a shared situational context is the very point of writing.

Halliday (1985) argued most forcefully, from an evolutionary point of view, that the construction of meaning in written language and speech works in fundamentally different ways. Writing and speech developed along very different lines and in response to diverse functional needs. It is, therefore, only to be expected that the underlying rules differ. Olson's (1977) article, programmatically entitled 'From utterance to text', contrasted the context dependency of situated speech with the unambiguous and self-sufficient representation of meaning in text. New research paradigms evolved, dedicated to the study of speech: from a sociological point of view, conversation analysis, and from a linguistic point of view, discourse analysis. Different in orientation as they were, they concurred that traditional categories of grammar, such as 'word' and 'sentence', were problematic and not necessarily suitable for the analysis of oral language (Gee 2005). In this connection Linell (2005) demonstrated that, notwithstanding the professed commitment to the priority of speech since de Saussure, the basic analytic concepts of linguistics are grounded in writing. Grammar describes language as a rule-governed system for the production of infinitely many complete sentences, but has no place for fillers, (*er/erm, well*), hedges (*or something, sort of*), backchannel signals (*uhuh, yeah*), lexicalized phrases (*whatsoever*), clitics (*nt* in *shouldn't*), routine formulae (*what's up?*), repetitions and other features of speech. Taking into consideration a number of conditions operating in conversation in contrast to writing, grammatical descriptions of spoken language have been proposed. The most important of these conditions as formulated by Leech *et al.* (1999) are:

- Conversation is interactive.
- Conversation is conducted in a shared situational context.
- Conversation takes place in real time.
- Conversation involves social relations and emotional attitudes.
- Conversations make use of a restricted repertoire.
- Conversation employs a vernacular range of expressions.

On this basis, Leech (1999) and his associates have pursued the project of an English grammar of conversation, with the declared purpose of correcting the grammarians' bias towards the written language. Their work embodies an unorthodox approach to grammar that highlights rather than downplays the differences between speech and writing.

Yet, while much evidence has been accumulated in support of a positive answer to the question of whether speech and writing follow different grammars, there has also been a backlash. Detailed surveys of differences between speech and writing have revealed that features deemed characteristic of one could also be detected in the other (Biber 1988). A speech can follow a script, and writing can be colloquial. Based on this observation, many linguists embraced the notion of a continuum of manifestations of spoken and written language first proposed in the 1980s (Tannen 1982). Instances of both spoken and written language, the continuum model suggests, can be rated along various scales such as intimacy–formality, involvement–detachment, personal–public, among others. In literate societies, the range of linguistic behaviour is far too multifarious to be described adequately by means of a unilinear continuum between two opposites, oral and written. This is certainly true, and, as we shall see in Chapter 7, it is likely that computer-mediated communication further contributes to blurring the dividing line between speech and writing, while adding yet more complexity, for formality grading is at work in both spoken and written language. However, it is not so obvious that abandoning the distinction between clear cases typifying oral and written language helps to advance our knowledge about what writing does to language and what it does to society.

It is also important to note that the notion of the oral–literate continuum as well as grammars for conversational speech were developed in the context of, and for the analysis of, language behaviour in highly literate societies, where, typically, 'literacy events' are not just embedded in 'oral events' (Heath 1982), but both are considered manifestations of the same language. Both the speakers of oral performance and the grammarians have experienced extensive exposure to writing. A grammar of a language that has no written form – to which, obviously, the notion of an oral–literate continuum is not applicable – is an altogether different matter. It is under such conditions that the second variant of our above question must be dealt with: 'Does the grammar of an unwritten language exhibit any features that set it apart from that of written languages?' The quote at the beginning of this chapter suggests a positive answer. Its author, anthropologist and linguist Giorgio Cardona, had much experience working with unwritten languages in Africa and was an expert on writing systems to boot. He speaks of the fluidity of speech not just in the sense that, obviously, the spoken word is ephemeral, while once put in writing it is fixed for re-inspection at will. In another, more profound sense, the spoken word is not as clearly recognizable a unit as it is when we look it up in a dictionary. Linguists working on the documentation of endangered languages offer a glimpse of what the problems are:

> In many literate societies, native speakers have relatively clear ideas about wordhood, but their perception of word boundaries is largely based on the orthographic conventions familiar to them.... In many non-literate societies, speakers are also able to segment utterances into form–meaning pairings of word-like sizes.... The consistency with

> which such segmentation is performed, however, varies greatly
> between individual speakers and speech communities. (Himmelmann
> 2006: 254f.)

Similar observations are reported by Christian linguists grappling with
the liturgical use of unwritten vernaculars: 'In the absence of writing
there are no means of insuring consistency' (Tanner 2004: 68). The variation and inconsistency in delimiting linguistic units – be they words or
languages – is what Cardona's (2009: 132) above-quoted remark on the
fluidity of unwritten languages is about. It leads us back to a point made
in Chapter 1 about the units of language being theoretical constructs
(see p. 7). Language documentation work confirms the influence of writing on these constructs: 'When people can use a dictionary to look up a
word, to see how it is spelled, and to read a definition, the speech community's authority over "proper" usage is irrevocably altered' (Haviland
2006: 160). And it is not just words that are problematic in unwritten
languages, but also higher-level units. Writing, inevitably, imposes a
structure which is not present experientially. Himmelmann's report on
having native speakers who are literate in a dominant language work
on transcriptions of their own, unwritten language is instructive:

> In the initial phase, the transcripts may often be difficult to interpret
> because they appear to be full of inconsistencies and lack of
> indication of higher level units (transcripts can go on for pages
> without a single punctuation mark or indention to show the
> beginning of a new unit.) Over time and usually influenced strongly by
> the practices of the researcher(s) or the dominant writing culture, a
> more consistent and 'orderly' set of transcription practices may
> emerge which in turn may feed directly into an emerging literacy in
> the speech community. (Himmelmann 2006: 254)

REDUCTION AND EXPANSION

What Himmelmann describes is the transition from orality to literacy
for a language and its speakers. This process has often been called,
especially by missionary linguists, 'reducing a language to writing'. 'In
what sense "reduce"?', we may ask. There are at least three answers to
this question. First, no piece of writing is a faithful visual rendition of
speech. It ignores tempo, variation of loudness, intonation, pitch and
other articulatory features, not to mention mime and gestures, and thus
is a reduction.

Second, it is a reduction also of the fluidity, variability, vagueness and
uncertainty of speech. Is *myself* one word or two, and what about *their*

selves? In writing, word boundaries are usually decided one way or the other; in speech, it may just depend. The range of possible meanings of an expression is reduced in writing, as words are assumed to have a hard semantic edge which allows us to ask, 'What is the *literal* meaning of this term?' – a question that does not make much sense in speech, and certainly not in unwritten languages. 'Is this a sentence, I wonder?' Like the word, the sentence is not such a clear-cut category in speech as in writing. As Abercrombie (1963: 16) remarked, 'the sentence as traditionally defined is really a unit of prose, not of conversation'. Arguably, the sentence is a unit of written language. Even in languages that have had a written form and a literate speech community for centuries, sentences in speech and writing are not quite the same: 'Sentences in speech are much more loosely constructed, much less tightly packaged or integrated, than in writing' (Gee 2005: 132).

Finally, establishing a written form is a reduction in the sense that it reduces the range of associated varieties, drawing boundaries between languages. Cape Dutch was a substandard variety of Dutch until it was given a written form and a reference grammar in its own right in the early twentieth century; it was from then on called Afrikaans (Willemyns 2003; Deumert 2004). Writing, unlike speech, prompts the question: which language? The fluidity of speech areas described as dialect continua, such as continental West Germanic, Romance and Slavic, is divided into languages by virtue of writing.

The process of providing a language with its first writing system in modern times must not be confused with the invention of writing, for those who go about reducing a language to writing are literate and bring to it literate models of how language works that, as Himmelmann put it, 'feed into an emerging literacy of the speech community'. Thanks to these cognitive models and the historically evolved instrument of the Roman alphabet that is commonly employed to this end, it is all but impossible to develop an unbiased written form for a hitherto unwritten language. The result of such an exercise is a reduction.

However, furnishing a language with a written form is not only a reduction, but also an expansion. With writing a greater range of stylistic variation emerges, as well as new genres, such as the word list that grows into a dictionary, the novel and the codex, to mention but a few obvious examples. Writing, then, is a tool for language development. The concepts of *Abstandsprache* and *Ausbausprache*, first introduced by Kloss (1967) in order to come to terms with the problem of drawing a boundary-line between language and dialect, are useful in this connection. Different vernaculars qualify as languages for two different reasons. One is structural and lexical distance (*Abstand*): 'An abstand language is a linguistic unit which a linguist would have to call a language even if not a single word had ever been written in it' (Kloss 1967: 29). There are no closely related varieties with which it is mutually intelligible. Thus many African languages spoken in close proximity, but genetically unrelated, are languages by abstand. In contrast, an ausbau language qualifies as such by virtue 'of its having been shaped or reshaped ... in order to become a standardized tool of literary expression' (Kloss 1967: 29). It is made fit for all domains, including education, law and cult, by deliberate and more or less systematic lexical enrichment and grammatical standardization. Afrikaans, which, as mentioned above, split from Dutch by ausbau, is a case in point. Many languages are languages on both counts. French, German and English, for instance, are sufficiently distant from one another not to be confused with one another, but have also been subject to ausbau for centuries. Other languages, such as Croatian and Serbian and the Czech and Slovak languages, form dialect continua, but opinion leaders of the respective speech communities decided to increase the distance between their languages by developing their own ausbau processes. The principal instrument for this is writing. There is no – and there cannot be an – unwritten ausbau language, for writing is instrumental in demarcating boundaries, in the form of different orthographies or writing systems, and in accumulating a reference corpus of 'authentic' language.

DIGLOSSIA

The result of ausbau is not necessarily the substitution of vernaculars by one unified cultivated language. In fact, more commonly the ausbau language arises in addition to and coexisting with vernacular speech forms. Where there is strong divergence between the two and a clear division of functional domains is upheld, the language is said to manifest *diglossia*, from Greek δύο 'two' and γλοσσα 'tongue'. Originally developed for the literary variety of Modern Greek by Krumbacher (1902), the concept was introduced to sociolinguistics by Ferguson (1959), who singled out Greek, Arabic, Swiss German and Haiti Creole as paradigm cases of diglossia. Fishman (1967) diluted the concept somewhat by associating diglossia with bilingualism, arguing against reserving the concept for the co-ordinated use of genetically related varieties. Many different types of diglossia have been distinguished since, reflecting both diverse sociolinguistic environments and theoretical points of view and definitions (Schiffman 1997; Hudson 2002). As the concept has been applied to various languages with their distinct histories and ecologies and multilingual situations, its definition has become blurred but it is still useful to describe the habitual use of two or more varieties of the same language throughout the speech community with complementary functions. These varieties are labelled 'high' (H), used for the purposes of writing and formal speech, and 'low' (L), used for ordinary conversation. For instance, in the Arabic-speaking world, the language of the Qur'an ossified into C(lassical) A(rabic), H, which was handed down from one generation to the next with few changes, while spoken dialects, L, continued to evolve, giving rise to increasing divergence. Diglossia is an integral part of Arabic linguistic culture, which comprises a complex set of beliefs to the effect that H is more elaborate and rule-bound, more logical and more beautiful, while L is considered unregulated but intimate. Owing to the origin of H in the holy book of Islam, religious associations also play an important role. CA is a carrier of tradition and 'socializes people into rituals of Islam, affirms their identity as Muslims and connects them to the realm of purity, morality, and God' (Haeri 2003: 43). A learned language, CA is far removed from the mother tongue of any Arabic speakers, which is why arguments have been put forth and attempts have been made to use regional varieties of Arabic, such as Egyptian, Syrian and Moroccan Arabic, for writing. However, another layer of complexity is added to Arabic diglossia by the pan-Arabic appeal of CA as a unifying feature of the Arabic world. As a result, while a new variety for writing centred on Egypt, Modern Standard Arabic (MSA), has evolved, CA is still considered the supreme form of the language. What is more, MSA is also far removed from Arabic vernaculars, but, like colloquial varieties, it is 'to a large extent unpredictable and thus ill defined' (Kaye 2002: 124).

On the Indian subcontinent, too, diglossia is so widespread that it seems to be a fundamental characteristic of the linguistic culture. There are studies of diglossia in Bengali, Sinhalese, Kannada, Tamil, Telugu and Malayalam, among others. There is, furthermore, 'a tendency to develop diglossia even in languages that originally may not have exhibited a great degree of it' (Schiffman 1997: 212). This was true of Hindustani when it was chosen upon independence as India's national language. The vernacular was considered too vulgar by many intellectuals, who took pains to develop an H variety by taking recourse to Sanskrit literature. Since ancient times, Sanskritization of many written languages of India has driven a wedge between a literary variety and the vernacular spoken by the man in the street (Deshpande 1979: 99). Tamil diglossia, described in great detail by Britto, is a case in point. L comprises 'primarily spoken and conversational varieties and contrast[s] with the literary and classical varieties' (Britto, 1986: 130). Gair describes Sinhala diglossia in similar terms:

Literary Sinhala. The chief defining characteristic is Literary main verb forms, particularly the subject-verb agreement lacking in other varieties... It should be noted that this is the variety characteristic of virtually all written Sinhala, not just of literature per se.

Spoken Sinhala, lacking Literary verb agreement, but with two main varieties, *formal spoken* ... and *colloquial,* the language of ordinary conversation. (Gair 1986: 324)

By way of interpreting the social and cultural significance of Sinhala diglossia, Gair emphasizes two observations: (1) the overall level of literacy in Sri Lanka is very high, and (2) H and L in Sinhala show few signs of convergence, a point also made about Tamil diglossia by Britto. This is important, for, while the social cleavage between a literate elite and the illiterate masses characteristic of pre-modern societies is fertile ground for a linguistic cleavage to emerge between written and unwritten language, speech communities sometimes retain a sociolinguistic arrangement with grammatical and status distinctions between H and L in spite of universal literacy, as witnessed by the Swiss-German and Sinhala diglossia. In both environments, the introduction of literacy into a society created an environment particularly conducive to diglossia. However, the spread of literacy as an accompaniment of modernization did not bring about the end of diglossia. Universal literacy notwithstanding, the Swiss have maintained an H/L distinction between *Schriftdeutsch* and dialects for generations, as also seems to be the case in Sinhala, Tamil and other Indian diglossias. It also holds for Arabic diglossia: 'Saudi Arabia, for example, has become a modern state over the past half century, yet diglossia still permeates the society. It has not declined nor is it now in a state of declining' (Kaye 2002: 124).

Diglossia is not a natural situation, but a historically contingent artefact, like writing, and is strongly associated with writing. Standard Finnish, which was the subject of intensive ausbau activities in the nineteenth century, combines elements of various dialects. It was deliberately created for use in writing and, except in formal orations, is rarely used in speech. Standard Indonesian, elevated to the status of Indonesia's national language in 1945, is likewise a cultivated variety (H) used in writing. In daily conversation native speakers of Indonesian use an array of dialects (L) interspersed with aspects of other local languages that are, accordingly, more or less distant from the standard variety and from each other. In contrast to L, H is a normative variety that is subject to monitoring and cultivation. Lexical innovation in H is less spontaneous than in L, often drawing on the resources of a classical literary language, such as Classical Sanskrit, Classical Greek and Classical Chinese, which have a long tradition and a rich body of literature.

Borrowing from other languages is often frowned upon in the context of H, which, because of its link to an idealized archaic form of the language, tends to be associated with an ideology of purism. A good example of this is the 'purifying' H variety of Greek, Katharevousa, created in the early nineteenth century, a compromise between Classical and Modern Greek. By virtue of harking back to archaic grammar and lexis it was deemed more suitable for the literary, juridical, administrative and scientific purposes of the newly formed modern Greek state than the allegedly corrupted vernacular, Dimotiki, L, which included many Turkish and Arabic loan words. Since then, demotic Greek has been declared Greece's national language, in 1976, causing Katharevousa to lose ground. It has been argued, therefore, that the Katharevousa–Dimotiki split is relevant to the discussion of diglossia only until the early twentieth century: 'Since then, the Greek sociolinguistic situation can be analysed through the use of other approaches, such as Bernstein's relation of linguistic codes to symbolic control' (Frangoudaki 2002: 106).

If Frangoudaki's analysis is correct, the history of Modern Greek exemplifies a point made earlier: diglossia is an artefact. It comes and goes, even though it can become a part of the linguistic culture and persist for a long time. To capture the dynamic aspect of diglossia, various approaches have been suggested, culminating in the notion of a 'diglossia continuum' (Schiffman 1997), which undoubtedly does justice to the great array of sociolinguistic situations that over the years have been discussed under the heading of diglossia. By looking in depth at individual cases, we gain more understanding of the many ways in which different varieties are charged with different functions, are allowed or made to develop in different ways, or coexist in a situation that is stable or has entered a volatile phase after having been perpetuated for a long time. For present purposes, however, a detailed breakdown of the many kinds of diglossia is less relevant than the general features.

What the four paradigm cases of diglossia identified by Ferguson (1959) – Arabic, Greek, Swiss-German, and French and Creole in Haiti – and all major cases analysed subsequently have in common is that H is a cultivated variety with a codified written standard. This is not to deny that L is occasionally used in writing, nor that in some unwritten languages there exists a highly stylized variety used for ritual and other formal occasions. In any specific case of diglossia, the division of labour between H and L is subject to modulation by the structure of social domains, stratification (social class, caste), literacy and level of education. Thus every diglossia exhibits some unique features, but, as illustrated by the examples discussed here, it is invariably H that serves for writing and formal speech, while L is used in informal settings. Since L is spoken by everyone, it is not the variety of the illiterate; but H is the language of written communication. To be sure, there are overlaps and the H/L division is not equally rigid in all diglossia situations. However, in the final analysis, diglossia is an outgrowth of the introduction of writing into human communication. It is not a necessary consequence of writing and literacy, but a factual one.

This should be recognized. That it is not, and that after fifty years of research and debate 'diglossia' stands out as one of the key notions of sociolinguistics for which there is no generally accepted definition, epitomizes the theoretical weakness of the field. It is partly due to the ill-informed handling of writing as derivative of and subordinate to speech. Diglossia is testimony to the fact that the functional differences between oral and written communication brought about by the introduction of writing have a formative influence on language, rather than just on its uses.

Table 3.5 *Spoken and written language*

Spoken language	Written language
speech	writing
discourse	text
sound	image
dialect	standard
vernacular	prestige language
restricted code	elaborated code
patois	language
Mundart	Ausbau language
colloquial	learned language
low variety (L)	high variety (H)

CONCLUSION

The distinctions between written and unwritten language reviewed in this chapter have highlighted the effects of writing on society and on language. In sociolinguistics various conceptual frameworks have been used to capture particular aspects of these distinctions, which can be summarized as in Table 3.5.

The contrasted concepts in Table 3.5 are not interchangeable or parallel. They accentuate different aspects of the written/unwritten divide and do not necessarily identify mutually exclusive categories. Dialect features may find their way into written prose, by design or unwittingly.

'Oral literature' and 'eye dialect' – non-standard orthography used to typify a character in literature – are not considered oxymorons by those studying these language forms. Oral performances, such as in news broadcasting, prepared announcements, scripted speeches and staged dramatic productions are voiced texts; and substandard writing has been part of literacy in everyday life for many people. Vernacular speech, dialect, restricted code, a conversation in L, etc., can all be put into writing. But the point is that these are marked cases. Most writing in the British context for which Bernstein (1966, 1971) developed these notions is closer to the elaborated code than to the restricted code. It is pointing out the obvious to state that spoken language is realized in speech. Usually people do not articulate as on stage. It takes professional training to do that. And written language manifests itself in texts, not necessarily in a prestige language or learned variety, but typically the production of texts is guided by a standard. Major frame conditions such as the presence or absence of shared knowledge, vision and situation are taken into consideration in planning conversational interventions and written messages; failing that, contributions by speakers and writers are perceived as deviant, marked or deficient, for in literate societies, there are clear ideas about the differences between spoken and written language, varying in detail from one society to another, but congruent in many respects, since writing is *not* visible speech but an extension of the communication habits limited to orality. Table 3.5 encompasses the major differences that have grown out of the coexistence of and division of labour between spoken language and written language. The specifics of communicative practices that have come into existence in the wake of literacy are dealt with at greater length in Chapter 5; but first we will take a closer look at what it takes for a society to become fully literate and how literacy relates to the social order.

QUESTIONS FOR DISCUSSION

1 Fill in the matrix in Table 3.1 for a language of your choice and discuss the reasons for completing it as you did.

2 Calvet, quoted by Marfany (2010: 5), describes an old lady who, he says, 'speaks Occitan and thinks she speaks patois'. Marfany's comment about this description is as follows: 'What the old lady knows and Calvet apparently does not, is that, when she speaks patois, she speaks patois, not a language; when she wants to do that, she speaks French.' Discuss the differences between Calvet's and Marfany's understanding of the notions 'language' and 'patois'.

3 'A word is what is written between spaces.' Discuss this definition and what it implies for the analysis of speech.

4 Can the language resource matrix be applied to the H and L varieties of a language that exhibits diglossia separately or in combination? Try to find a suitable case and discuss the problems.

Resources / Reference group	Intellectual	Cultural	Emotional–symbolic	Social	Economic
World					
Nation					
Ethnicity					
Organization					
Family					
Individual					

H as a resource

Resources / Reference group	Intellectual	Cultural	Emotional–symbolic	Social	Economic
World					
Nation					
Ethnicity					
Organization					
Family					
Individual					

L as a resource

4   Literacy and inequality

The valuation of literacy is a significant factor for understanding how the state determines the nature and extent of democracy. (Creppell 1989: 25)

LITERACY IN THE PUBLIC SPHERE

Having established the major differences between spoken and written language, we can now return to the social significance of writing, in particular to its function for the public sphere. In Chapter 2, we saw that the seeds of the public sphere were already sown in the Greek city states of antiquity, where a 'separation between the public and the private person' (McGuigan 1996: 147) developed and writing became part of the communication ecology. It was the reification of the message in writing that made the dissociation of content and transmission an experiential reality for the educated elite. From then on, writing furnished the foundation on which grew Europe's culture of rationality, of examining texts for their inherent merit and consistency irrespective of the author, a culture that appealed to reason rather than emotion.

In this spirit the public sphere is the sphere of rationality. In retrospect its modernizing function is associated with overcoming the absolute power of the monarch in pre-modern Europe, with enlightenment and the emergence of bourgeois society, and with democracy. Habermas (1991: 32) pinpointed 'the golden age' of the public sphere in the half-century between 1680 and 1730. The public sphere was then the realm of social life where private citizens assembled, free from state supervision, to engage in rational argument and debate beyond personal interest and circles of acquaintance. It would seem that the public sphere requires as a precondition a literate community ready to receive information in the absence of an informer, a message that has an originator who, however, is not co-present with the recipient. The arrival of the printing press in the mid fifteenth century and the spread of printed matter it brought about paved the way for the Enlightenment movement and the modern culture of impersonal knowledge and informed judgement (Eisenstein 1979). It is therefore somewhat surprising that, in the literature on the public sphere, literacy plays only a marginal role. The public sphere, where rational–critical debate could unfold, was said to originate in the coffee houses of London and in Paris salons. The first newspapers as a means of giving expression to public opinion that was not officially authorized opinion were an important element of the sphere that came into existence mediating between the state and society. But in the eighteenth century the ability to use the information made available in newspapers and other printed matter was severely limited, literacy being far from universal. Yet, in Habermas' conceptualization the public sphere is all-inclusive: 'Access is guaranteed to all citizens' (Habermas 1974: 49). This, however, never meant that everybody had access. For one thing, citizenship was narrowly defined, excluding large parts of the population. 'Access to all' was an idealization, true only in the sense that, as opposed to feudal society in which one's life was largely determined by birth, the emerging bourgeoisie offered a wider range of life chances – though hardly access to all.

To be fair to Habermas, we must not forget the subtitle of his original book about the public sphere: *An Inquiry into a Category of Bourgeois Society*. The public sphere in its ideal form stood – and fell – with bourgeois society, potentially open to all, but factually limited to the middle class consisting of educated and propertied persons who could partake in the discussion of serious matters such as literature, economics and politics. It was open in the sense of not excluding anyone by predetermined criteria of birth. Yet it was an exclusive sphere limited to citizens who could read. In the eighteenth century, this meant educated affluent men. The public sphere in Habermas' sense was the sphere of 'high culture'.

Today, the public sphere is both more comprehensive and fragmented, having become commercialized, trivialized, trashy and invaded by special-interest groups who appeal to their own clientele rather than to the general public (McKee 2005). It has become more egalitarian, to be sure, but access for all is still a normative value rather than an actual fact. Literacy is a good yardstick to demonstrate how exclusive the public sphere has always been and continues to be. To engage in sustained debates about matters of public interest, literacy at a higher than elementary level is a prerequisite. Printed matter intended for wider circulation was at the heart of the public sphere when it first evolved; active participation in this sphere furthermore presupposes the ability not just to read and understand texts, but to contribute by supplying suggestions, interpretations and commentaries. This ability was very unevenly distributed in bourgeois society and still is in today's society; for while the specific meaning of literacy keeps changing, it continues to be an element of inequality. In what follows we will track the complex relationship between the spread of literacy and the development of the public sphere by looking at this relationship from the point of view of social inequality. Literacy made the public sphere possible, but at the same time it established cultural capital (Bourdieu 1984) as an effective means of making distinctions within society and controlling participation in the formation of public opinion, which became an ever more important constituent of modern societies.

The dimensions of inequality to be considered are social stratification, race, gender, and language and ethnicity. It is no coincidence that this list mirrors the variables that were foregrounded one after another as sociolinguistics took shape as a field of scientific study. They all stood in the way of universal literacy and exemplify the more general point that cultural capital, like financial capital, is distributed inequitably and not all members of society have equal access to societal goods. This is so because in modern capitalist societies their distribution is regulated by institutions that mediate between the forces of the market and moral norms of social justice. The former are predicated on the imperative of profit maximization, and reward success and financial gain, thereby inevitably amplifying economic inequality and power differentials. The latter feed into the design of institutions meant to counteract these tendencies and to protect the less powerful against the destructive dynamics of the capitalist mode of social organization which subsume both practical and intellectual skills as well as social relations under the 'laws of capitalist accumulation' (Streeck 2010). Considering literacy in an institutionalist framework against this background, the following question arises: *What institutions provide literacy to whom, to what end, and at what cost?* Institutions are organizations characterized by rules designed by rule makers and followed by rule takers (usually including the rule makers). In modern societies, as opposed to pre-modern ones, where literacy was closely associated with the institution of the church, the institutional provider of literacy is the school. However, despite the universalist ethos of general education and the right to participation in social organization, the school has not been able to eradicate economic and social inequality. Recognition of the fact that these inequalities have a bearing on how people speak is at the heart of sociolinguistics. They also have a bearing on how they write and what they read. Viewed in this light, literacy is indicative of the social condition.

SOCIAL STRATIFICATION

Article 25 of the Universal Declaration of Human Rights stipulates that 'everyone has the right to education. Education shall be free, at least in the elementary and fundamental stages. Elementary education shall be compulsory.' Assuming that compulsory education aims to produce a literate populace, this aim is yet to be fully realized. The OECD Programme for the International Assessment of Adult Competencies (PIAAC) defines literacy as 'the ability to identify, understand, interpret, create, communicate and compute, using printed and written materials associated with varying contexts. Literacy involves a continuum of learning in enabling individuals to achieve their goals, to develop their knowledge and potential, and to participate fully in their community and wider society.'[1] Even in the affluent OECD countries, sizeable population segments do not meet this standard. Functional illiteracy continues to be a problem. In today's society it is a problem because 'inequalities in literacy contribute to inequalities in income, occupational status and access to certain labour markets' (Movement for Canadian Literacy n.d.).

The social stratification of literacy skills we observe today is an old legacy (Graff 1986), for those who knew how to read and write had control over the flow of written information in society from early on, and the more important the exercise of power through writing became, the weightier became their influence. Learning to read and write has always been tied to privilege and social advantage. The connections between literacy and social stratification are bidirectional: social class has an influence on the distribution of literacy skills, and the consumption and production of written material are indicative of social class.

Literacy and poverty statistics tend to be closely related. This is why adult literacy, defined as the ability to engage in all those activities of everyday life in which reading and writing are required, is part of the United Nations Human Development Index (HDI). This index applies not just to developing nations but to all nations, and, although there are cultural differences that translate into different attitudes towards literacy, there is a general positive correlation between literacy rates and wealth, social status and power. The 2008 HDI report includes the values given in Table 4.1 for people lacking functional literacy skills for a select number of the most highly developed countries.

Since the standards of functional literacy differ from country to country, comparable data are hard to come by. Literacy rates obtained for some countries just reflect primary and secondary school enrolment, while others use survey data. The UNESCO Institute for Statistics (UIS)

Table 4.1 *Functional illiteracy and low income in selected OECD countries*

Country	Population lacking functional literacy skills (%)	Population below 50% of median income (%)
Sweden	7.5	6.5
Norway	7.9	6.4
Netherlands	10.5	7.3
Finland	10.4	5.4
Denmark	9.6	5.6
Germany	14.4	8.4
Switzerland	15.9	7.6
Canada	14.6	11.4
Australia	17.0	12.2
Belgium	18.4	8.0
United States	20.0	17.0
United Kingdom	21.8	12.6
Ireland	22.6	16.2

Data from Human Development Index 2008, http://hdr.undp.org/en/.

obtains literacy statistics for people aged fifteen and older from national population censuses, household surveys and estimates, trying to develop international standards (UNESCO UIS 2010). Literacy rates reflect cultural, social and regional differences as well as stages of economic development. What is more, in addition to the difficulties of comparing different national educational systems, the stigmatization of adult illiteracy in advanced countries is a problem for the collection of reliable data. However, it is clear from all available statistics that adult illiteracy, low income and low social status go hand in hand. Poor and disadvantaged families are overrepresented among functional illiterates, and people with literacy problems are more likely than others to have low-paying or no jobs and to be at risk of falling into poverty. The very condition of functional illiteracy means that information about welfare and literacy training programmes often does not reach those who need such programmes most.

Table 4.1 shows that insufficient literacy in advanced countries is not a matter of the past. The International Adult Literacy Survey (OECD 1997, 2000) presented further evidence of the magnitude of literacy problems in the OECD countries, problems that will be exacerbated as ever more jobs in these societies become dependent not just on the

Table 4.2 *Consumption of two newspapers by socioeconomic status*

Socioeconomic status	Percentage of the *Sun* readership	Percentage of *The Times* readership
A (highest income and level of formal education)	1	16
B	6	41
C1	18	26
C2	35	9
D	26	5
E (lowest income and level of formal education)	15	3

Source: Sparks 1991, quoted in McKee 2005: 73

possession of reading, writing and numeracy skills, but on technological abilities in an information-based economy. The critical threshold of competence in the knowledge society keeps rising, as does the risk of social exclusion for those with below-standard functional literacy. As Barton (1994: 196) put it: 'Ultimately literacy reflects inequalities in society: inequalities in power, inequalities in the distribution of wealth, and inequalities in access to education.' In the most advanced countries, education authorities have been trying to overcome the problem for decades, and they have been assisted by many non-state actors, such as the Movement for Canadian Literacy, which spells out the rationale for the fight against adult illiteracy:

> Literacy is, itself, a defining characteristic of social class. Literacy is an instrument of social power. People become part of a culture by learning to interpret and use its particular signs and symbols. They use language in social relations that increase their knowledge and develop their potential. Poor literacy skills can exclude people from the dominant social groups and opportunities in a society. (Movement for Canadian Literacy n.d.)

The 'signs and symbols people learn to interpret' – that is, the kind of written language they consume, if any – are also subject to social stratification. A socioeconomic breakdown of the readership of two British newspapers suffices to illustrate the point. One is the 'easy-to-read' tabloid *Sun*, and the other is *The Times*, an upmarket broadsheet.

The difference between *The Times* and the *Sun* can be described in terms of taste, but taste, as Bourdieu (1984) has taught us, is a matter of social class. Thus, the strikingly inverse stratification of the readerships of the *Sun* and *The Times* is another manifestation of the fact that literacy is a predictor of socioeconomic status. At the bottom, people with poor literacy face serious difficulties in the labour market. In democratic polities this is nowadays generally recognized as a defect that must be corrected, for the ideological commitment to enlightenment and equality that is so strongly rooted in these societies is not compatible with inequities of this sort. This was not always so, as the use of literacy requirements as an instrument of exclusion from political participation indicates.

RACE

The public sphere is predicated on a literate community who partake in the formation of public opinion and take notice of it. An informed public is considered by writers about the public sphere to be essential for democracy to work. People who vote must know what they are voting for, and since a great deal of relevant information is distributed in writing, literacy is a necessary condition for political participation. Or so the argument goes. Because, in Western thinking since the Renaissance enlightenment, equality, freedom and democracy have been ideologically linked to each other, this argument is quite persuasive. Francis Bacon's adage 'knowledge is power!' has convinced us all, and what value is knowledge if it is not written down?! India is an obvious counter example to the conjecture that democracy requires literacy, since, upon independence from British rule in 1947, the right to vote was extended to all citizens, even though the overall literacy rate was only about 16 per cent at the time (Creppell 1989; Premi 2002). The political fathers of India's independence decided that a Westminster-style government was worthy of emulation, but they took pains to decouple political participation from literacy, as the illiterate masses the British Raj had bequeathed to them would have been excluded. To this day, pictorial symbols of the political parties are therefore printed on the ballots (Figure 4.1).

However, in many Western countries when, after the French Revolution, the notion of universal (male) suffrage gained ground, imposing education-based restrictions on the right to vote needed little justification. Just as children were excluded from suffrage rights, so were uneducated people. In the nineteenth century and throughout the first half of the twentieth, it was thus widely held that suffrage rights should be made contingent on the capacity to read and write. Unlike tax and property criteria, literacy requirements were seemingly egalitarian, as

	Indian National Congress (INC)
	BSP Bahujan Samaj Party (BSP)
	Bharatiya Janata Party (BJP)
	Samajwadi Party (Socialist Party) (SP)
	Nationalist Congress Party (NCP)
	Communist Party of India (CPI)

Figure 4.1. Political party symbols allowing illiterate Indians to cast their vote

they were imposed on all citizens.[2] It took a while to realize that literacy requirements served to limit the electorate much as property qualifications did.

Creppell (1989) has analysed the introduction of literacy tests as a condition for exercising suffrage rights in the United States during the latter decades of the nineteenth century after the Civil War. The major purpose, especially in the Southern states, was to bar former slaves from going to the polls. Before abolition, in clear recognition of the subversive potential of literacy, the enslaved Blacks were never taught to read and write, and their literacy level was accordingly extremely low. Literacy tests, some of which were very difficult, involving the reading of sections of the US Constitution or other legal documents, were a convenient means of disenfranchising the former slaves under the guise of a general requirement to be met by all citizens: 'The veneer of impartiality attached to literacy tests allowed racist voting practices while deceiving the more naïve public' (Creppell 1989: 31).

African Americans were not the only group targeted by literacy tests as a restrictive device. Uneducated poor peasants driven en masse across the Atlantic from Ireland by the Great Famine (1845–52) were also, and intentionally, affected by this policy; however, the battleground of the fight against the use of literacy tests to restrict voting was race relations. The nexus of literacy and race came to the fore in conjunction with the

Civil Rights Movement in the USA. The Voting Rights Act of 1965 finally outlawed poll taxes and literacy tests as a precondition of registering to vote. This did not diminish the appreciation of literacy in American society, but it made American democracy more inclusive.

Raising the literacy level of the group that until then had been denied suffrage on grounds of insufficient literacy was another matter, for reading and writing are not just technical skills but a cultural practice which in modern societies is key to social advancement (Gee 1990), but to which different ethnic groups are differently accustomed (Heath 1981). In the United States, literacy levels differentiate ethnic groups to this day. To what extent this must be attributed to cultural preferences or differential access to printed matter, technology and other resources is a hotly debated question. Auerbach (1992) has called for a critical reassessment of the correlation between literacy and economic mobility, arguing that an individual's life chances depend more on race and gender than on the acquired facility with the written word. The fact is that a White–Black gap in reading achievement persists (Corley 2003). One in-depth study investigated the literacy programme of Baltimore, Maryland, a predominantly Black city. In their closing comments, the authors quote former Mayor Kurt Schmoke, an African American, who in his inaugural speech said that his greatest ambition was to make Baltimore 'a city that reads'. They come to the conclusion that during his time in office this aim was not accomplished, for, despite the great importance accorded to literacy education in Baltimore, '38% of the city's adults still read below the sixth-grade level as of 2001' (Serpell, Baker and Sonnenschein 2005: 277). In the United States, African Americans stand out as the ethnic group with the lowest literacy level (Jencks and Phillips 1998), and disadvantaged ethnic minorities in other countries similarly come out at the bottom end of literacy assessment tests. For instance, Australia's Indigenous Literacy Project (n.d.) reports that, by the age of fifteen, more than a third of Australia's indigenous students do not have sufficient literacy skills to meet the requirements of everyday life; and, according to Statistics New Zealand (n.d.), literacy skills of the Maori population are significantly poorer than those of the White population. The conditions of literacy and educational attainment differ from country to country, and it is not always easy to isolate race/ethnicity from social status. However, in advanced countries where race is an issue, low literacy levels tend to be a good predictor of race, poverty and low social status. Thus, even in advanced countries, the Enlightenment project of universal education of all children in literacy is yet to be fully realized, as differing literacy rates of ethnic groups are testimony to the fact that universality was curtailed by race not too long ago.

Explanations for the White–Black literacy gap have been sought in material and cultural circumstances, such as limited access to print by students of colour in their home, but linguistic factors have also been adduced. In the American context it has been argued that African-American Vernacular English (AAVE) is a dialect, creole or language so different from Standard American English (SAE) that literacy education in SAE puts African-American students at a serious disadvantage. In the 1980s and 1990s, fierce ideological battles raged about whether African-American students should be taught to read and write in AAVE or, on the contrary, African Americans should strive to modify their speech so as to narrow the gap between their own variety and SAE and thus facilitate the learning of written English (Ball and Lardner 2005; Redd and Schuster 2005). Since this debate is to do with questions of identity and language rights, no disinterested solution can be expected. In the present context it is of interest because it leads back to the discussion in Chapter 3 about diglossia, patois, dialect and standard language and the question of what variety is to be used in writing.

The classic question of sociolinguistics is: who says what in what language to whom where and to what end? If we apply this question to written communication, the nexus of literacy and race adds a double layer of complexity to it, highlighting the fact that this question is not one of free choice, as choices are restricted by social frame conditions. For it is not just 'who writes what...?', but also 'who *can* write?' And the question of 'in what language?', too, is socially determined, for not all languages are considered legitimate for written communication. Rather, the functional distribution of languages/varieties and their acceptability for writing are as much part of a society's power structure as is the distribution of literacy skills across groups. Besides race, the most conspicuous variable in this regard is gender.

GENDER

Historically, women everywhere trailed behind men in the drive for universal literacy. In Renaissance Europe, for example, women's average level of education and hence their ability to read and write were lower than men's. Literacy skills are still distributed unevenly between the sexes virtually everywhere, as is evident from illiteracy statistics: an estimated 64 per cent of the world's adult illiterates are female. The less developed the region, the higher the gender disparity of illiteracy, and it is more acute in rural areas than in urban ones. For instance, the male–female gap in adult literacy in Sub-Saharan Africa is 18 per cent, and in South Asia it is as high as 22 per cent, as of 2008 (UNESCO Institute for Statistics 2010b). Literacy work in developing countries is therefore closely linked with women's empowerment campaigns. Malini Ghose of the Nirantar Centre for Women and Education in New Delhi put it bluntly: 'As feminist literacy practitioners...our concern has been explicitly with changing power relations at a social and individual level' (Ghose 2001: 296). The point of departure for these practitioners is the potential of written language as a tool not just for the acquisition of knowledge but also for the analysis of power relations and the distribution of resources in society. It is in rural areas of developing countries that literacy education most obviously works as a force of social change. India is the prime example of concerted efforts to overcome illiteracy in rural areas. Women have played a critical role in designing, executing and participating in campaigns for 'total literacy'. And women came to the realization that mere literacy as a technical skill was not enough, but that literacy campaigns needed to be integrated into programmes for adult education that are sensitive to cultural differences and aim at delivering literacy skills that have practical utility for the population concerned. In India, since 'adult education could not be divorced from attempts to bring about social change, the programme was renamed social education' (Dighe 2000: 324). Other organizations such as ASP-BAE, the Asian South Pacific Bureau of Adult Education, and Bunyad in Pakistan have similarly moved away from focussing on literacy only towards a more comprehensive concern with adult education.

This is much in keeping with the approach of the 'New Literacy Studies', which favours the notion of literacy practices focussing on the nexus of literacy and power and the ideologies associated with literacy campaigns. In India and other developing countries, literacy instruction is a sociopolitical task helping women to connect better to wider society and to reflect on their own lives, thus enabling them to play a more active and informed role in planning their life course. Literacy in these contexts is a force that challenges traditional social patterns. In fact, in many communities the idea of gender equality, arrived together with literacy programmes. Yet even in countries whose governments have embraced gender equality, a literacy gender gap persists. For instance, Djité (2011) reports that in Cambodia, Laos, Myanmar and Viet Nam literacy rates for females, both reported and tested, are well below those of males. Similar gender discrepancies are found in Latin-American countries (van der Westen 1994). Literacy campaigns sponsored by UNESCO, therefore, employ a gender-based approach targeting primarily women. These campaigns are closely tied to basic services such as education and health for people living in poor areas, where high levels of illiteracy correlate with maternal and infant mortality (see, e.g., UNESCO 1998). The expectation is that literacy will help women in these disadvantaged rural and urban areas to improve their understanding of reproductive health, strengthen their self-esteem and, by spreading the value of education, break the perpetuation of poverty from one generation to the next.

The gender gap in poor areas of developing countries is aggravated by another factor: minority languages that are ignored in school curricula and adult education programmes. Low social status, gender discrimination and ethnic minority affiliation combine to form the highest hurdle that literacy projects designed to promote social justice must overcome. The ethno-linguistic diversity of many countries further illustrates the complexity of social, cultural, economic and political aspects of the ambitious goal of making all members of society capable of dealing with written language at a level that is adequate to cope with the demands of everyday life. Before we look at the linguistic dimension of literacy, an additional remark about the links between literacy, gender and attainment serves to underline the contingency of the traditional gender gap in education and the sometimes unexpected nature of social change.

Over the past half-century, the gender asymmetry in the most advanced countries has not only been reduced but turned on its head: a significant majority of the functional illiterate adult population are men. For instance, according to a 2010 survey, in Germany 14.5 per cent of the working-age population between 18 and 64 years are below the level of functional literacy. Of those, 35.8 per cent are women and 64.1 per cent men (leo 2011). The French national agency for the fight against illiteracy reports an illiteracy rate of 9 per cent of people aged 18–65, of whom 41 per cent are women and 59 per cent men (ANLCI 2005). In Britain, 16 per cent of the population 16–65 years old have a literacy level of or below that expected of an 11-year-old.

Furthermore, the new gender disparity in the adult population is mirrored in the schools. Nowadays, boys' underachievement in literacy is a matter of concern in some Western countries. In Britain, girls outperform boys in all categories of literacy, i.e. English, reading and writing (Jama and Dugdale 2010). Lee (1996) argues that gender roles in the classroom let 'boys talk and girls listen'. According to her analysis, girls' superior literacy skills are likewise to be attributed to the construction of differing 'gender subjectivities' and gender dynamics in the classroom. Taking an ethnographic approach along similar lines, Moss (2007) analyses hierarchies of readers in class, taking into consideration how attainment is affected by group size, physical space, teachers' postures, permission for pupils to move around, etc.

These studies among others lend credence to the New Literacy Studies in that they demonstrate how the acquisition and effectual promotion of literacy skills depend on cultural patterns, hierarchies and social expectations and attitudes from which literacy practices ultimately derive meaning. These patterns and attitudes concern in no small measure the languages of writing and their writing systems.

LANGUAGE AND ETHNICITY

In Europe the promotion of popular literacy since the Renaissance coincided with the transformation of pre-modern sociolinguistic arrangements in which the differences between oral and written communication typically coincided with linguistic differences. Most notably, the preeminence of the three holy languages of Christianity, Hebrew, Greek and especially Latin, as the principal languages of writing was undermined and eventually eliminated by the enlistment of many other languages for literary purposes. In pre-modern multilingual Europe the written language was for the overwhelming majority of the people far removed from what they spoke. The dominance of Latin in the wake of Roman colonization and Christianization produced two types of functional division. In what is today the area of the Romance languages, the written language was related to but became increasingly divorced from the spoken language, and in Celtic-, Germanic- and Slavonic-speaking areas the principal language of writing was unrelated to the vernaculars. At the threshold of modernity, various coinciding developments led to a narrowing of the gap, as vernaculars were written down and literacy was extended to a wider section of the population. However, the megatrend of breaking the monopoly of Latin as the language of rule, religion and learning never meant that 'anything goes' – that is, that any kind of speech was deemed fit to be written. Bourdieu's concept of 'legitimate language' (Heller 2001), to which we had occasion to refer in Chapter 1, encapsulates the problematique at issue here.

The dominance of Latin was challenged in the name of, and in conjunction with, erecting alternative power structures, as the Roman Empire which Latin served as an overarching bond disintegrated and nations established themselves as political entities. As a result many *national* languages were established as legitimate languages, equipped with their own writing systems and orthographies. In institutionalist terms, 'legitimate language' means a language that enjoys some kind of official backing. Through its employment in education, government announcements and other official functions, that language becomes an institution in its own right, a development which culminates in the sanctioning of violations of recognized spelling rules. The gradual increase of formal education brought the written language closer to the masses, who were taught it was their language they had to learn to read and write. The rise of national languages as vehicles of education broadened the demographic base for mass literacy, but at the same time created new divisions and new inequalities. In order to make them fit to compete with Latin and to assume similar functions, they were modelled on Latin, its grammar and regulated spelling (Harris 1980), and their standardization was enforced as a means of political control. In present-day parlance, national language formation and nation building went hand in hand. Teaching a particular form of the language played an important role in fostering intellectual and moral integration and building 'the common consciousness of the nation' (Bourdieu 1991). After the French Revolution, as ever wider segments of the population were drawn into school, the educational system 'no doubt directly helped to devalue popular modes of expression, dismissing them as "slang" and "gibberish" . . . and to impose recognition of the legitimate language' (Bourdieu 1991: 49).

Associated with power and learning, Latin enjoyed high prestige which, through the nationalization of education, was transferred to the national language. This caused minor languages and dialects to slide down the prestige hierarchy almost everywhere in Europe, for general education, both for ideological and for practical reasons, employed the legitimate language. Local dialects and minority languages came to be associated with backwardness and provincialism. In the case of France, the connections between modernity, education and the delegitimization of local forms of expression were particularly clear. Lartichaux describes the linguistic situation in France prior to the revolution as follows: 'The power speaks French and it cares little about the fact that the mass of the populace continues to speak the local language' (1977: 68f.). The revolutionaries equated linguistic fragmentation with an unbridgeable gap between rulers and ruled, while the 'unity of the idiom was an integrating part of the Revolution' (1977: 68f.). National unification and the elimination of privilege were equally important objectives of the French Revolution, and in time the eradication of local patois came to be seen as part of the package. Parisian French was to be promoted as the language of the new Nation together with egalitarianism, rationalization and uniformization. Thus French became the legitimate language of general education and of writing for all purposes. The press, Lartichaux (1977: 82) observes, was 'carefully placed in the front rank of the battle to create an official language in an official literature', that is, Bourdieu's 'legitimate language', which was already the language of the public sphere in which other languages had no place.

In many ways the French language regime is paradigmatic for modern nation states. With very few exceptions they are multilingual, but priority is given to the national language, which is the language of government and education charged with the task of building the nation and holding it together. The modern state embraced an ethos of monolingualism and imparted literacy to the populace in the legitimate language, while minority languages were seen mainly as threats to unity and political harmony. The national language was a symbol and vehicle of progress, while regional dialects and minority languages alike were perceived as, and thus turned into, leftovers from times past. They were portrayed as uncouth, boorish and generally inferior to the classical languages as well as the literary languages of modernity. The latter shared with the former the prestige that comes with officialdom, culture and formal education. In a highly centralized state such as France, it was long considered self-evident and thus hardly ever disputed that such prestige could not and should not be accorded to minority languages.

The consequences of the modern policy of granting legitimacy to one language over all others are still reflected in today's literacy rates of ethnic minorities, both indigenous and immigrant, which tend to be lower than that of the majority whose first language is the legitimate language. Heightened awareness of the problem of language discrimination and its ideological implications for democratic polities only gained ground as of the mid twentieth century, when UNESCO adopted the principle of promoting mother tongue literacy. Literacy campaigns along these lines were targeted primarily at developing countries, in many of which the legacy of colonial languages as principal written languages proved to be a major obstacle to mass literacy promotion. However, against this background, calls for equal rights for minority languages in Western countries became ever harder to ignore. That all children should be taught to read and write in their mother tongue, except for children of language minority groups, is clearly incongruent with an egalitarian ideology.

With the adoption in 1992 of the European Charter for Regional or Minority Languages, whose stated aim it is 'to ensure, as far as reasonably possible, the use of regional or minority languages in education and the media and to permit their use in judicial and administrative settings, economic and social life and cultural activities', Europe has turned a page in dealing with ethnic and linguistic minorities, adopting a post-modern approach that differs from that of the modern nation state in being more pluralistic and inclusive. Yet the question of what language is to be used for literacy education is far from being settled. Language regimes die hard, and for many children throughout Europe home language and school language continue to be different. As was discussed above, this gap also has a social dimension, the speech of middle-class children being closer to the school language than that of working-class children; and regional dialects, too, are at variance with the school language. However, while children raised in a Swabian small town, in the French Pyrenees or in the West Midlands do not enter school speaking standard German, French or English, respectively, their speech is much closer to the school language than that of their Turkish, Algerian or Pakistani immigrant peers.

The growth and increasingly felt presence of new immigrant minorities in the affluent countries of Western Europe have contributed to raising the level of attention paid to lingering literacy problems in these societies. It has become clear that the drive towards universal literacy, which overlapped with the institution of national languages, has produced a new kind of inequality between those who are taught reading and writing in their mother tongue or a variety close to it and those to whom literacy comes in a foreign language. Attempts to redress this imbalance, or rather to compensate for it, have only been made sparingly in a few countries that have set up special literacy programmes for ethnic minorities (Extra and Verhoeven 1992).

The problem of providing literacy to members of ethnic minorities in plural societies has several dimensions. First, there is the issue of granting recognition (legitimacy) to a group and its language. Whether Kurdish is a legitimate language in Turkey, Iraq or Iran is a question that is qualitatively different from that of whether it is a legitimate language in Sweden or Germany. There are some 60,000 Kurds resident in Sweden and 10 times that number in Germany, but that does not automatically imply a recognized status for the Kurdish language in these countries, where its presence is of recent origin. If a state accepts the principle of universal compulsory education and subscribes to the notion long promoted by UNESCO that a child should be taught to read and write in his or her mother tongue, does it follow that the state is obliged to deliver literacy to all of the mother tongues spoken in its territory? Hardly, if only because that would be impractical. There are other reasons, too, why governments abstain from or reject literacy education in minority languages, such as lack of funds, and lack of educational materials and teachers, as well as ideological reasons. Compulsory education is still seen by many as an instrument of social engineering and nation building. Delivering literacy to all in the national language(s) is given priority over mother tongue literacy virtually everywhere. Growing immigrant populations in the affluent countries of Europe and North America have highlighted the issue in recent years (Wiley 1996; Extra and Verhoeven 1992). In several countries, legal residency and work permits have been made contingent on proving competency in the national language by answering multiple-choice questions, in the national language, on the history, culture and law of the country in question. In the name of integration immigrants are required to pass tests in the national language. While governments in many countries from Britain to Italy enact such programmes in the name of integration intended to foster mutual understanding and help immigrants get ahead in society, there is also concern that literacy requirements are effectively a tool to stem the tide of immigration. That is not far-fetched and lends further support to the notion that literacy must be understood as an integral part of the power structure of society.

Next, there is the issue of utility, which is of paramount importance in capitalist society. Clearly, literacy in the dominant language has utility for immigrants, but whether or not literacy in their language of origin has any utility for their children very much depends on the status of that language. For instance, does literacy in Akan help Ghanaian immigrants in Italy make a living? In Ghana, English is the dominant language of literacy, and most Akan immigrants from Ghana are bilingual. Since they come to Italy primarily in pursuit of economic gain, literacy in Akan is not a high priority for them, although they are much attached to their native language for symbolic reasons of identity and intimacy (Guerini 2006). Hence, there is no more pressure to gain support for literacy education in Akan among Ghanaian immigrants in Italy than there is in Ghana where, as in many other African countries, linguistic homogenization is promoted in the name of economic development (Djité 2008). What we see at work here are the forces of the capitalist mode of socioeconomic organization that tend to expand marketization to all spheres of life, including language (Coulmas 1992).

The function of the state in capitalism is to contain market expansion by building institutions that protect weaker groups and correct the distorted allocation of resources. In the most advanced countries, various measures of minority protection have been established in the course of the last half-century. On the whole, assimilation pressure on indigenous minorities has lessened as a result, and more languages have gained recognition in school curricula within the wider context of multicultural education. The consolidated European nation states can afford to be generous to their indigenous and, to a lesser degree, their immigrant minorities. Yet, as part of the dynamics of capitalist development, there is a constant tug of war between the imperative of utility and the marketization of social life, on one hand, and the defence of non-economic interest, on the other. The promotion of mother tongue literacy must be understood in this context (UNESCO 2008). Market forces accelerate linguistic homogenization leading to the spread of some big languages at the expense of many small ones. Mother tongue literacy, quite apart from the pedagogic advantages it allegedly entails, is seen by many as a safeguard for minority languages under pressure. This is why there are still minorities with some members who reject the concept of a division of labour of the languages co-present in a society that entails that only one or some are used in writing, and who aspire to written status for their languages instead. These include languages that lack a written standard, such as Friulian in north-eastern Italy (Coluzzi 2007: 203ff.), Alsatian in eastern France (Broadbridge 2000), Guernsey French (Sallabank 2002) and Galician in Spain (Beswick 2007: 229). Others are bent on re-establishing their language in lost functional domains – for example Low German, which in the course of the seventeenth century was replaced as a written language by High German (Becker-Cantarino 1988). These are just some examples, and they do not begin to illustrate the great variety of sociolinguistic configurations involving minority-language literacy.

It is because of this variety that sociolinguists, developmental psychologists and literacy researchers have taken up the issue; for it stands to reason that children who learn to read and write in a foreign or second language have to cope with the double task of learning the unfamiliar language and the ways of the written word (Sassoon 1995; Cook and Bassetti 2005). Whether and to what extent this is a serious impediment for literacy learning is not an easy question to answer. Nowadays, against the deeply rooted ideology of mother tongue education, there is a strong tendency to answer it affirmatively. Some studies have indeed shown that second language learners lag behind their monolingual peers in assimilating reading and writing routines (Verhoeven 1987), but general conclusions cannot easily be drawn because the cases of non-native-language literacy for children and adults are highly diverse, involving different languages, different writing systems and population groups of different ethnic and social backgrounds. The matrix in Table 4.3 encompasses some of the relevant variables.

For instance, Sorbian, a Western Slavic language, is an indigenous minority language in Eastern Germany spoken by some 50,000 people. It has a written standard making use of the same writing system as the neighbouring dominant languages, German and Polish. The Latin alphabet is augmented with a couple of digraphs and a diacritic not

Table 4.3 *Minority-languages literacy*

Written status Minority status	Written standard	Same writing system as dominant language	Different writing system from dominant language	No writing system
indigenous				
immigrant				

Setting: A national state or region

used in either of these languages. Sorbian is formally taught in some local schools. By contrast, Romansh is an indigenous minority language in Switzerland that has never developed a unified standard and whose regional idioms have five differently coded written forms, all using the same writing system as the surrounding dominant language, German (Tessarolo and Pedrotti 2009). Kurdish in Sweden, Germany and other European countries is an example of an immigrant minority language that has no unified written standard. It is native to several regions in Iran, Iraq, Syria, Turkey and former USSR republics and is variously written in modified versions of the Arabic alphabet, the Latin alphabet and the Cyrillic alphabet. This poses obvious problems for providing literacy in Kurdish to Kurdish immigrants in European countries. Yet another case is that of Chinese as an immigrant language abroad. The city of London, for example, has a community of some 100,000 Chinese residents, many of them hailing from Hong Kong. Their primary language is Cantonese, which is used in writing (Snow 2004), although it is more common for Cantonese speakers to use Mandarin Chinese for written purposes. In any event, the writing system is structurally completely different from that of the dominant language, English, although children in China also learn to read Romanized Chinese, *pinyin*, mostly for pedagogical purposes. As these few examples illustrate, there is a great diversity of combinations of language and writing system in minority contexts involving first and second language acquisition, and possibilities of transfer from one language and/or writing system to another, all of which raises many questions adding to the complexity of literacy education.

Constellations of the sort exemplified in the previous paragraph are typical of immigrant countries. In addition it must be kept in mind that conditions for providing literacy in minor languages differ significantly between these and late industrializers. The former have driven linguistic homogenization to the most advanced level, while at the same time making more funds available for the promotion of educational activities that cannot easily be justified in economic terms. In the latter countries, mother-tongue-based literacy education is often not part of official educational policy and the languages of ethnic minorities are hardly visible in the schools. It appears that the marginalization of minority languages that is most advanced in developed countries is being replicated along similar lines in late industrializers. Linguistic diversity is thus transformed into a pecking order of languages, while literacy education for ethnic minorities creates or reinforces inequality.

CONCLUSIONS

Mass literacy is a defining feature of modern society. In this chapter we have seen that it is conducive to promoting a higher level of participation and equality. At the same time, it has been used, and to some extent still functions, as a criterion for differentiating variously defined groups, thus introducing new inequalities. In modern society, universal education was promoted as a matter of necessity in order to produce a workforce capable of meeting the requirements of industrial production and the socioeconomic order of industrial capitalism. These requirements change as the economic needs of the capitalist social order evolve. The spread of literacy across social classes, gender, race and linguistic boundaries is testimony to the role of the state in social development. While the market produces the kind and level of literacy that is commensurate with the economic necessities at hand, the state serves as the principal agent for redistributing cultural capital.

The persistence of levels of functional illiteracy between 10 per cent and 15 per cent in the world's wealthiest countries suggests that, although the advancement of technology requires ever higher degrees of skill and literacy, the economic order of post-industrial society is not incompatible with an underclass lacking access to cultural capital, although the political ethos of equal opportunity is (Willms 1997). In a nutshell, this is one of the contradictions of late capitalism, especially in its neo-liberal guise, that call for state involvement in order to realize the liberating potential of literacy and mitigate the reproduction of inequality from one generation to the next – for, in modern society, rather than being a technical skill that is the preserve of specialists, literacy is a precondition of economic opportunity and full participation in society.

QUESTIONS FOR DISCUSSION

1 What was the rationale for introducing literacy requirements for voting, and for rescinding them?

2 If there is a correlation between literacy rates and per capita GNP across countries, and educational achievement has pay-offs in terms of individual income levels within countries, who should pay for literacy education as an investment?

3 What is a 'legitimate language', and what does literacy education have to do with it?

4 What does the principle of universal compulsory education enshrined in the Universal Declaration of Human Rights imply with regards to the state's obligation to provide literacy in minority languages?

5   The society of letters

*The advanced forms of human civilization, like universities and
like governments and like national elections – all of those require
writing.* (John Searle 2005)

WRITTEN LANGUAGE IN INSTITUTIONS

The institutions of modern society depend on writing and many are associated with a particular variety of written language. Taken together they
constitute the society of letters as a community. This chapter examines
three institutional settings which define frame conditions for certain
kinds of connections to come into existence and certain kinds of communicative behaviour to take place: government, religion and school.
Modern society is based on the dissociation of word and speaker by
means of writing. Rare is the day when people do not interact in writing
with public institutions, educational authorities, economic agents or
religious bodies. Institutions as we know them have a history and write
their own history by producing new documents every day. No government can function without rules and laws laid down in writing; without
issuing directives, statements and explanations; without drawing up a
budget and justifying expenditure. In religions, based on a holy text, the
written word has a normative function in relation to the sermon and
other oral expressions of faith. Although 'the three Rs' is a somewhat
dated notion, the very existence of the institution of school is predicated on the need to instruct pupils in the arts of reading and writing,
which, unlike oral language, are not usually acquired spontaneously.
Many institutions are largely defined by documents such as statutes,
contracts, bills, invoices, promissory notes, account ledgers, payslips,
tax forms, scriptures, prayer books, curricula, primers, examination
rules, term papers, dissertations and diplomas.

Institutions establish their own rules, codes of conduct and linguistic
conventions, and their written output is indexical of them, much as

speech varieties are indexical of an individual's social class, gender or regional origin. In many post-colonial settings, some institutions articulate themselves in the colonial language, manifesting in this manner their linguistic identity. For instance, in Mozambique, the official language is Portuguese, which fewer than 10 per cent of the people consider their mother tongue. Legal and administrative documents are published in Portuguese. Thus, for most people, officialese is literally a different language. However, even in settings where the vast majority of the people speak, and are schooled in, the same national language, an ossified, convoluted and pompous style that resists the innovating influence of informal varieties is the hallmark of institutional language. As in speech, the distinguishing features of institutional writing are an expression of, and fulfil, certain social functions. In the case of legalese, our first example, this is particularly apparent.

GOVERNMENT: LETTER VERSUS SPIRIT

The rule of law means that no one is above the law and that individuals cannot be penalized except for clearly defined violations of existing laws. It also means that statutes must be consistent. Statutes promulgated in writing must not contradict one another or certain general principles laid down in a constitution or fundamental law. Over the centuries this notion developed to become the cornerstone of legitimate rule in modern states, bringing in its wake a culture of exegesis, interpretation and the never-ending quest for precision of terms. The administration of justice in modern states is grounded in writing. Preliterate cultures were not lawless, but law as an objectified institution that is independent of the judge comes into existence with writing, as do many communicative activities that are derivative of, or refer to, the code. Some scholars, therefore, consider 'unwritten law' an oxymoron, and even defenders of the idea of a constitution that is based on unwritten principles do not deny that justice in contemporary society presupposes a large body of written text. Laws, testimonies, expert opinions, verdicts, appeals and confessions must be laid down in writing. The rule of law in our present understanding cannot prevail in the absence of writing. However, the foundations of bureaucratic government were laid much earlier.

The oldest state law is the Code of Hammurabi, King of Babylon, mentioned in Chapter 2. It consists of 282 statutes addressing commercial transactions, principles of contractual relationships, property and family matters such as inheritance and paternity – that is, all sorts of matters that are still subject to legal regulation in our day. At the outset, the code establishes the source of its authority:

> When the lofty Anu, king of the Anunnaki, and Bel, lord of heaven and earth, he who determines the destiny of the land, committed the rule of all mankind to Marduk, the chief son of Ea; when they made him great among the Igigi; when they pronounced the lofty name of Babylon; when they made it famous among the quarters of the world and in its midst established an everlasting kingdom whose foundations were firm as heaven and earth – at that time, Anu and Bel called me, Hammurabi, the exalted prince, the worshiper of the gods, to cause justice to prevail in the land, to destroy the wicked and the evil, to prevent the strong from oppressing the weak, to go forth like the Sun over the Black Head Race, to enlighten the land and to further the welfare of the people.

Compare this with the preamble of any law on the books in the UK, for example the Sports Grounds Safety Authority Act 2011:

> BE IT ENACTED by the Queen's most Excellent Majesty, by and with the advice and consent of the Lords Spiritual and Temporal, and Commons, in this present Parliament assembled, and by the authority of the same, as follows: –

While not quite as elaborate and convoluted as the Babylonian antecedent, contemporary legislation continues to state explicitly the authority in which it is grounded, using to this end a 'dignified' style that is distinct from everyday speech. A constitution on which a polity is founded is a written document encompassing guiding rules and morals for shaping society. Constitutions are by necessity very general in nature and hence call for interpretation; and interpretation means potential abuse. This is the birthright of the legal profession, which is an accompaniment of constitutionalism. The dispute of *the letter of the law vs the spirit of the law* (Figure 5.1) is an integral part of it, and the fact that 'the spirit' is often seen as the nobler of the two testifies to a traditional undercurrent of suspicion of writing (not just of the fine print) in Western culture, as well as the view that writing is only a secondary representation. The Pharisees are people who put the letter above the spirit of the law and are disparaged for that.[1] 'Rules lawyering', also known as 'gaming the system', is seeking ways of following the letter of the law to foil its intent. Ever since the code of Hammurabi the problem of letter vs spirit has dogged government and the execution of the law, but in spite of strenuous efforts to draft legislation that is clear and unambiguous, the gap between the two has widened rather than narrowed. The historicity of language coupled with the inertia of institutions did not allow otherwise.

Figure 5.1 The letter of the law vs the spirit of the law

That legal codes have developed their own language to form highly complex systems consisting of many different parts that are inter-related in various ways is a side-effect of the quest for greater clarity to minimize the divergence of letter from spirit. Vagueness and ambiguity of terms must be avoided, which is not easy because (1) many words are imprecise and/or polysemous, and (2) common language is always in flux. To deal with these two problems, legal literature has developed into a genre in its own right. But the pursuit of precision and the avoidance of confusion have made it rather cumbersome and inaccessible to non-professionals. Tiersma (1999) provides a wealth of examples as well as a historical analysis of how its Latin and French heritage has informed English legal writing in the UK and in the colonies, too. Complaints about the opacity of statutes and other legal documents as well as the unintelligible verbosity of lawyers go back centuries, and although many lawyers regard pleas for plain language with disdain (Kimble 1995), campaigns for the promotion of clear drafting are initiated at regular intervals (Clarity 2002). Linguistic conservatism is widespread in the legal profession. The veneration of authoritative texts is quasi-religious, for archaic and intricate language is associated with importance, trustworthiness and exactitude. Legal language contains many ritualistic elements, such as the cry of the bailiff at the beginning of a court session – *Hear ye, hear ye, hear ye* – and fixed formulae in writing, e.g. *in witness whereof I have hereunder set my hand*. It is common practice to recycle entire phrases and sentences from one indictment, petition or opinion of court to another, because copying is easier than composing and because it reduces the risk of committing procedural errors. While it is safe to use customary phrasing, in the course of time these ready-made elements of older texts gather patina, making legal documents less accessible to the public. The legal profession is generally averse to linguistic modernization, because many legal texts are the subject of authoritative interpretations. Since laws are interrelated in substance as well as in phrasing, a change in the wording of one act could have unforeseeable consequences for other parts of the system.

Legal language is archaic not because obsolete laws remain on the books, such as the Metropolitan Streets Act 1867, which prohibits the driving of cattle through the streets of London. Rather, there is understandable reluctance to change the wording of existing statutes and a tendency to use established terminology in drafting new ones. Constitutions and statutes are written precisely because they are meant to last and, therefore, cannot be permitted to be tinkered with. But sticking to customary terminology is no safeguard against conceptual changes which inevitably come along with conquest, cultural changes, technological innovation, etc. The asynchrony of linguistic change and conceptual change becomes noticeable only with writing, which, unlike the fleeting word, suggests stability. Green's (1999) semantic history of the Middle English noun *trouthe* is a fascinating example. Investigating its ethical – 'true to his word' – theological – 'faithful' – and legal – 'bound by contract' – senses, he demonstrates how *truth* gradually assumed its modern sense of 'conformity to fact', while its antonym, *tresoun*, shifted from 'unfaithfulness' to 'crime against the state'. He makes a convincing argument that, for our purposes, is of particular importance: that these semantic changes were caused by and accompanied the growing importance of written language and its influence on legal culture and statecraft.

In his classic study *From Memory to Written Record*, Clanchy (1979) described how the transition from oral to literate culture shaped the English legal system and state bureaucracy. As permissible evidence before the court, a person's truth was supplemented by the factuality of documents, and as writs, bills, contracts, tenancy agreements, etc., gained importance, so did the meaning of words. The normal messiness of everyday language became ever less tolerable to the legal mind, which sought salvation by fixing professional definitions. This has advantages.

Defined terms reduce the risk of ambiguity, make the interpretation of statutes, contracts and other official documents easier, and increase the likelihood that similar wrongdoings will be penalized in similar ways. But fixing the meanings of terms inescapably leads to the emergence of a specialized lexicon consisting of terms which look like ordinary words but cannot be understood without instruction.

Award	The decision of an arbitrator.
Factum	An act or deed.
Party of the first part	One of the people entering into an agreement (in a written contract).
Prayer	Request for judgment, relief or damages at the conclusion of a petition.
Negative pregnant	???

The resulting jargon has provoked never-ending calls for plain language and organized efforts to cleanse official documents of unnecessary jargon. In an often-quoted article entitled 'Goodbye to Law Reviews', American law professor Fred Rodell pledged not to contribute any more to legal literature, because, in his opinion, two things were wrong with it: 'One is its style. The other is its content' (Rodell 1936: 38). This is a rather sweeping indictment, but examples that prove him right are not hard to find. Consider a clause such as the following, which is contained in many legal agreements: 'The masculine shall include the feminine, the singular shall include the plural, and the present shall include the past and future tenses' (quoted from Freedman 2007: 3). This is about language, and it tells us that a number of linguistic distinctions that presumably evolved for a purpose can be dispensed with in legal language. Many scholarly disciplines use their own terminologies and phraseologies. The trouble with legal language is that full participation in modern society presupposes, even requires, knowledge of the law. *Ignorantia legis neminem excusat* is a principle from Roman law that purportedly is basic to our legal system. It means 'ignorance of the law excuses no one' and, as part of contemporary legal culture, is still often quoted in Latin. Participation in modern democratic societies requires citizens to be informed about their rights and duties. Yet, in the course of the centuries, legal jargon has drifted away from everyday language, with the result that it has become ever more difficult to abide by this principle.

Some of the features of legal language have already been mentioned, such as archaic and unusual vocabulary, e.g. *aforesaid, same, such*. Others include the preference for the passive voice and impersonal constructions, *it is required, this court finds*; phrasal verb constructions such as *place a limitation on, make an examination of* and *are in compliance with* rather than *limit, examine* and *comply with*; long complex sentences; and the avoidance of pronouns. In everyday speech pronouns abound, but because of their deictic nature, which makes them refer to different individuals in different contexts, they are less frequent in written texts and shunned in legal literature for fear of causing confusion. To some extent these devices help to reduce ambiguity, but they also contribute to making legal literature a hermetic maze that only specialists enter without fear of getting lost. The uninitiated depend as much on the counsel of lawyers as the unlettered in pre-modern times needed them to translate Latin or Law French. Consider an arbitrarily selected section of the aforesaid Sports Grounds Safety Authority Act as an example.

Part 1
SPORTS GROUNDS SAFETY AUTHORITY
1 Football Licensing Authority to become Sports Grounds Safety Authority
(1) The body established by section 8 of, and Schedule 2 to, the Football Spectators Act 1989 – (a) is to continue in being, but (b) instead of being called the Football Licensing Authority is to be called the Sports Grounds Safety Authority.
(2) Schedule 1 contains further provisions relating to the Authority.
(3) The expenses of the Authority are to be paid by the Secretary of State.

2 Advice to Ministers of the Crown
(1) The Authority – (a) may provide relevant advice to a Minister of the Crown, and (b) if requested to do so by a Minister of the Crown, must provide relevant advice to that Minister.
(2) 'Relevant advice' means – B *Sports Grounds Safety Authority Act 2011 (c. 6) Part 1 – Sports Grounds Safety Authority*
> (2) (a) advice in relation to safety at sports grounds generally, or (b) advice with respect to the exercise of any of the functions of the Minister in question under the enactments specified in subsection (3).

(3) The enactments are – (a) the Safety of Sports Grounds Act 1975, (b) Part 3 of the Fire Safety and Safety of Places of Sport Act 1987 (safety of stands at sports grounds), and (c) the Football Spectators Act 1989.
3 Advice to bodies or persons in England and Wales
(1) The Authority may provide advice relating to safety at sports grounds in England or Wales to – (a) local authorities, or (b) subject to subsection (2), other bodies or persons. (2) The Authority may not under subsection (1) provide advice to – (a) a Minister of the Crown, or (b) a body or person specified in section 4(1)(a), (b) or (c).

4 Advice to bodies or persons outside England and Wales
(1) The Authority may, if the conditions in subsection (2) are met, provide advice relating to the safety of sports grounds to – (a) the government of a territory outside the United Kingdom, (b) an international organisation, or (c) a body or person not falling within paragraph (a) or (b) whose functions, activities or responsibilities relate in whole or in part to the safety of sports grounds outside England and Wales.
(2) The conditions are that – (a) the provision of the advice is at the request of the body or person concerned, and (b) the Secretary of State consents to the provision of the advice.

5 Supplementary
(1) The Authority may, with the consent of the Secretary of State, charge a fee for the provision of advice under – (a) section 4 (advice to bodies or persons outside England and Wales), or (b) if the advice is provided at the request of the recipient, section 3 (advice to bodies or persons in England and Wales).
(2) A fee charged under subsection (1) must not exceed the cost of providing the advice.
(3) Fees received by the Authority by virtue of subsection (1) are to be treated for the purposes of section 1(3) as reducing the expenses of the Authority.
(4) A consent under section 4(2)(b) or subsection (1) may be given – (a) generally, (b) in relation to any particular advice, or (c) in relation to advice of a particular description.
    Sports Grounds Safety Authority Act 2011 (c. 6)
        Part 1 – Sports Grounds Safety Authority
(5) In this Part – (a) 'local authority' and 'sports ground' have the same meaning as in the Safety of Sports Grounds Act 1975 (see section 17(1) of that Act), and (b) 'Minister of the Crown' has the same meaning as in the Ministers of the Crown Act 1975.

Except for a few official terms such as *Minister of the Crown*, this law poses few terminological or grammatical difficulties. Yet it is not easy to understand what it is all about, because it is very long-winded, refers to other Acts, and contains a considerable number of subsidiary specifications. Clearly, no one speaks like that. Notice also that a need is felt for the draft itself to explain the meaning of the terms used (in 2(2) and (4)(5)). These are ordinary words rather than technical terms, but for the sake of clarity it must be spelt out what they refer to and that the intended meaning (referent) has not changed since the law was first drafted or last amended. It is also common for statutes to contain clauses such as this: 'In subsection (4)(b) above 'the appropriate manner' means – (a) if the person was given a fixed penalty notice, the manner specified in the fixed penalty notice, and (b) if he was handed a conditional offer,

the manner specified in the written receipt under subsection (2) above'
(UK Road Safety Act 2006). Thus, statutes and regulations both contain
internal explanations and are subject to external commentaries and
annotations, all in the interest of clarity. But clarity is not always
what is achieved. Commenting on the exaggerated confidence in the
precision of legal language on the part of lawyers, Tiersma (1999: 85)
remarks: 'The huge number of lawsuits each year over the meaning of
some word or phrase in statutes and other legal documents, virtually
all written by lawyers, is reason enough to question the legendary
precision of legal language.'

The difficulties of understanding legal documents are, of course, not
just linguistic. Legislation in modern societies is highly intricate, each
statute being part of a complex system. Much more is involved than
a good command of the vocabulary and grammatical knowledge. Both
in statutory law and in case law it takes years of study to acquire the
necessary knowledge of how the system works. Since ever more spheres
of life are regulated by law and new fields of human activity such as
cyberspace keep coming into existence, the subject matter of statutes
can be very complicated, as is reflected in the subdivision of law into
a considerable number of specialized branches. The division of labour
characteristic of contemporary advanced societies is such that we rely
on professionals for a great number of undertakings, including legal
affairs. The specialized nature of the necessary knowledge in law and in
other professions and trades implies a specialized language register.

PLAIN LANGUAGE

However, this hardly means that the opacity of legal language is due only
to the complexity of the subject matter. Other mechanisms are at work
as well to engender and maintain linguistic distinction. Institutions
have a tendency to sustain themselves which is aided by a language
that outsiders find impenetrable. Legal terminology has its practical
utility justified in the complexity of the subject matter, but it is also
employed to protect turf. The high social status enjoyed by the legal
profession rubs off on the language, which in turn is used to convey
an aura of authority and superiority, if not to intimidate and dominate
clients. Institutionalized law claims the right to stake out an area of the
common language for its own purposes, over which it rules.

Legal language has thus evolved into a load-bearing pillar of a profession that modern society cannot do without, with its own dictionaries,
glossaries and style manuals. Like Humpty Dumpty, writers in the

wonderland of law insist that 'When I use a word it *means* just what I choose it to mean – neither more nor less.'[2] Linguists may think otherwise, but for them there are only the crumbs that fall from the master's table, that they can pick up by way of making suggestions for plain drafting. Although many lawyers are inclined to think that only lawyers are qualified to reform legal language,[3] many reform panels, including official bodies charged with making government publications easier to understand, count linguists and communication experts among their members.[4] Thus one profession creates problems that allow another to make a living by trying to solve them. This, too, is an example of how writing affects the social division of labour. There is in democratic societies a persistent tension between the imperative that every citizen should comprehend the law and the need to use clearly defined terms that do not deviate from established legal usage. Professional lawyers are quite aware of this tension, as is exemplified, for example, by a resolution adopted by the American Bar Association. On 9 August 1999 the House of Delegates resolved

> That the American Bar Association urges agencies to use plain language in writing regulations, as a means of promoting the understanding of legal obligations, using such techniques as:
>
> • Organizing them for the convenience of their readers;
> • Using direct and easily understood language;
> • Writing in short sentences, in the active voice; and
> • Using helpful stylistic devices, such as question-and-answer formats, vertical lists, spacing that facilitates clarity, and tables.
>
> To avoid problems in the use of plain language techniques, agencies should:
>
> • Take into account possible judicial interpretations as well as user understanding;
> • Clearly state the obligations and rights of persons affected, as well as those of the agency; and
> • Identify and explain all intended changes when revising regulations.
>
> (American Bar Association 1999)

In its first part the resolution urges agencies to use easily understood language, but in its second part it emphasizes the importance of paying heed to judicial interpretations and makes some other suggestions to avoid problems in the use of plain language. As for the first part, linguists may have something to contribute to improving the comprehensibility of legal texts, but the second part reminds us that legal language is also a technical language which requires specialized knowledge if it is to be manipulated without jeopardizing the purpose it serves. It was a success for the plain language movement that the US Senate passed the Plain Language in Government Communications Act (Senate Bill 2291), but empirical research has shown that plain language is only slowly gaining acceptance in legal drafting (e.g. Wheatman and LeClercq 2011).

RELIGION: THE ALPHA AND THE OMEGA

The Law is not the only institution that asserts authority over language and breeds a caste of officials who identify with it and use it for special purposes, including their own benefit. Organized religion is another. If this were a historical book, cult would have been dealt with before the previous section about law, for legal codes are generally grounded in a religious tradition. But our interest is more in the communication domains of contemporary society and the functions they assign to writing than in history.

Scriptures change the nature of religious culture by fostering the differentiation of the sacred and the profane and, in many cases, by elevating one language above others to become the language of sacred texts and liturgy. *Bible* means 'book', from Greek *biblion* 'scroll', and since antiquity *people of the book* are the adherents of a faith based on scriptures. In Judaism the term refers to the Jewish people, and Muslims use it to refer to followers of Judaism and Christianity, the Abrahamic religions that preceded the teachings of the prophet Muhammad. In the Indian context, after the Islamic conquest, Muslims granted both Hindus and Buddhists the status of *people of the book*. The Roman Catholic church prefers the term *word of God* rather than *Book*, but other Christian denominations freely use *people of the book*, much like their Jewish and Muslim brethren. To leave no doubt about the fundamental importance of writing, the people of the book identify the deity itself with it, the beginning and the end, which in the literate mind extends from alpha to omega.[5]

It is not just Judaism, Christianity and Islam that are inextricably bound up with book culture. The authority of scriptures is also a formative element of Buddhism, Hinduism and other book religions. From the point of view of monotheism, Buddhism and Hinduism are sometimes described as philosophies rather than religions; however, in spite of theological differences, the veneration of certain fundamental texts is socially comparable with the function of holy books for the religions of Semitic origin. For example, the Lotus Sutra and the Vedas have for many centuries served as the foundation of an edifice of doctrines, interpretations and commentaries that have been passed down from one generation to the next. The conservative language attitude that grows out of the notion of text as divine revelation is another commonality associated with religious culture. Sacred languages include: Biblical Hebrew as the language of the Talmud – a word that means 'teaching'; Latin as one of the three holy languages of Christianity (Hebrew and Koine Greek being the other two); Old Church Slavonic in the Russian Orthodox Church; Sanskrit, the eternal language of Hindu scriptures as well as Mahayana Buddhism; Pali, the original language of Theravada Buddhism; Classical Chinese for Mahayana Buddhism; Classical Arabic, the language of the Qur'an, the only miracle of Islam; and Ge'ez, the revered language of Ethiopian Jews and Christians.

The association of some religions with more than one language in this list implies that, in the long run, no language is so sacred that it cannot be replaced or supplemented by others. This is particularly apparent in the multilingual environment of South Asia, where, typically, 'one language is used to convey more than one religious system and one religious system is expressed through the medium of more than one language' (Pandharipande 1992: 271). Judaism and Islam have been most concerned with reserving expression of the dogma to one language only, Hebrew and Classical Arabic respectively.

Wherever a language is idolized as the medium of a heavenly message to the faithful and in which a body of sanctified texts is compiled, the impulse to protect it against deliberate change comes to the fore, as the transmitters and custodians of the doctrine establish the exact wording and standards of correctness, the medium being associated with the message. As a countervailing tendency, there is the desire on the part of the masses to understand what time and language barriers render incomprehensible to them. As a result religions have seen their own plain language movements advocating vernacularization or translation, both of which have brought new fields of intellectual and economic activity into being.

TRANSLATION

Of all religions, Buddhism has produced by far the largest corpus of sacred texts. Its emergence as a major world religion is a history of translation. In contrast to monotheistic creeds Buddhism has no inhibition or decree against translation; neither does it recognize the notion that one language is *the* true one. In the Kullavagga in the second book of the Theravadin, there is the following discussion between two Bhikkhus (monks) and the Blessed One about this question: 'At the present time, Lord, Bhikkhus, differing in name, differing in lineage, differing in birth, differing in family have gone forth (from the world). These corrupt the word of the Buddhas by (repeating it in) their own dialect. Let us, Lord, put the word of the Buddhas into (Sanskrit) verse.' The Blessed One had no patience with this suggestion, telling the monks that it would not be conducive to conversion. He said: 'You are not, O Bhikkhus, to put the word of the Buddhas into (Sanskrit) verse. Whoever does so, shall be guilty of dukkata [wrongdoing]. I allow you, O Bhikkhus, to learn the word of the Buddhas in his own dialect' (*Vinaya Texts* [1885]: 150f.). Thus, translation was not just permitted but actively promoted, and different canons resulted from major translations: the Pali canon, the Tibetan canon and the Chinese canon. With translation came schism, and with that the delimitation of religious sects and regions. Similar developments characterized the spread of Christianity. The Christian Bible is the most widely translated book in the world. In antiquity the Hebrew Bible was rendered into Koine Greek (Septuagint), Syriac, Coptic, Ge'ez and some other languages of the region. During the Middle Ages several translations from the Greek into other European languages were undertaken, such as the Gospel of John into Old English and the Gospel of Matthew into Old High German, both in the eighth century CE. A complete translation into Old French appeared in the late thirteenth century, and John Wycliffe's Middle English Bible a century later (1383). But the business of Bible translation really took off at the threshold of the modern age.

The churches of the Protestant Reformation were the driving force behind the production of vernacular Bibles, such as Martin Luther's German translation (printed in 1522), Christian II's Danish Bible (1524), the Dutch Bible by Jacob van Liesvelt (1526) and the most famous English-language translation, the King James Version, created by as many as fifty-four translators and published over 400 years ago, in 1611. Many others followed in the age of the European expansion, as Christian missionaries from Europe and North America swarmed across the globe. The Wycliffe Bible Translators were especially active, striving to make 'God's word accessible to all people in the language of their heart' (www.wycliffe.org/).

However, making a sacred text accessible in the vernacular (assuming that that is the language of 'their heart') opens a can of worms, to put it mildly. If there can be one translation, there can be many, and that imperils the integrity of the sacred text, creating what is known as 'the problem of competing authorities' (Jeffrey 1996: 175). The risk that a translation changes the meaning of the original ever so slightly has led to discussions, bans of 'unauthorized' versions of scriptures, conflicts, schisms and the whole problem of the meaning of meaning. Consider as an example some versions of the Gospel of John 1,1.

Latin

> In principio erat Verbum et Verbum erat apud Deum et Deus erat Verbum. (Biblia sacra vulgata)

English

> In the beginning was the Word, and the Word was with God, and the Word was God. (King James Bible 1611)

> In the beginning the Word already existed. The Word was with God, and the Word was God. (New Living Translation, 2007)

> From the first he was the Word, and the Word was in relation with God and was God. (Bible in Basic English)

French

> Au commencement était la Parole; et la Parole était auprès de Dieu; et la Parole était Dieu. (Darby Bible 1880)

> Au commencement était la Parole, et la Parole était avec Dieu; et cette parole était Dieu (Martin Bible 1744)

German

> JM anfang war das Wort, Vnd das Wort war bey Gott, vnd Gott war das Wort. Das selbige war im anfang bey Gott (Luther 1545)

> Im Anfang war das Wort, und das Wort war bei Gott, und das Wort war Gott. Dieses war im Anfang bei Gott. (Schlachter 1951)

Spanish

> En el principio ya era la Palabra, y aquel que es la Palabra era con el Dios, y la Palabra era Dios. (Sagras Escrituras 1569)

> En el principio existía el Verbo, y el Verbo estaba con Dios, y el Verbo era Dios. (La Biblia de las Américas 1997)

Minor differences, perhaps, but surely each translator will have compelling reasons why their version is preferable to others, and thus the stage is set for an endless round of arguments.[6] Entire libraries of commentaries have been written about this one verse allowing hosts of learned men – and men they usually were – to make a living by studying words and laying the foundation of theology and what Jacques Derrida called the logocentrism of Western philosophy. The words of John 1,1 are cryptic enough to allow for rival understandings to be proffered.

In his drama *Faust*, Goethe classically expressed the conundrum of
the proper translation, providing at the same time an example of
the amenability of word meanings to time and context. The Faustian
translation has been interpreted as opening a new period in European
history: modernity, a period that prizes action over contemplation.

> 'Tis writ, 'In the beginning was the Word.'
> I pause, to wonder what is here inferred.
> The Word I cannot set supremely high:
> A new translation I will try.
> I read, if by the spirit I am taught,
> This sense: 'In the beginning was the Thought.'
> This opening I need to weigh again,
> Or sense will suffer from a hasty pen.
> Does Thought create, and work, and rule the hour?
> 'Twere best: 'In the beginning was the Power.'
> Yet, while the pen is urged with willing fingers,
> A sense of doubt and hesitancy lingers.
> The spirit comes to guide me in my need,
> I write, 'In the beginning was the Deed.'
> (*Faust*, trans. Philip Wayne, 1962, Penguin Classics,
> Part I, p. 71.)

The point of departure of Faust's enigma is a *written* word, the Greek
word λóγος (*logos*). What does it mean? The translations quoted above
have by and large settled on 'word', but any Greek–English dictionary we
consult gives us both *word* and *thought* for λóγος. Since, in the puzzling
verse Ἐν ἀρχῇ ἦν ὁ Λóγος, καὶ ὁ Λóγος ἦν πρὸς τὸν Θεόν, καὶ Θεὸς ἦν ὁ Λóγος,
logos is moreover equated with God, its meaning seems to be rather pro-
tean, so why not *deed*, indeed?! This is Semantics, or soft semantics,
exegesis, interpretation, hermeneutics. Is the Faustian suggestion a personal gambit, or is it sanctioned by the polysemy of the Greek word
logos? There is a tension in this question between, on one hand, how
Faust intends to understand the word in its context, and, on the other,
how much leeway its 'dictionary meaning' allows him in this regard
with any degree of plausibility. For example, no classicist would permit
'In the beginning was a cup of tea' as a possible translation of John 1,1,
for 'a cup of tea' is just stretching too far the limits of what *logos* could
conceivably mean. Actually, it is not at all clear that tea was even known
to John the Evangelist, not to mention the fact that, as Scholastics will
doubtlessly point out, a cup of tea cannot have been at the beginning,
because first someone had to make tea. So this option is out. *Thought*, in
contrast, is a legitimate translation which makes a lot of sense, if you
are inclined to accept that thinking should precede speaking.

Faust's choice of *deed* as the proper translation clearly is the fruit of intense intellectual effort, for he was a very learned man. But did he care much about what John wanted to say? And should he have cared? Word meaning, author's intention and reader's interpretation may not coincide. Since we are dealing not with a crossword puzzle but with a holy book, bridging any real or apparent gap between the three is a matter of some consequence which is compounded through translation. The ensuing problems of heterodox interpretations, the Inquisition, burning people at the stake and so on could perhaps be sidestepped if translation of scriptures were proscribed and exegesis reserved to a small class of authorized experts.

Such an approach is preferred by devout Muslims, who do not accept translations of their holy book, the Qur'an, which they regard as a revelation from God in the Arabic language. The Qur'an is therefore intimately tied to the Arabic language and its alphabet, the script in which it was first written down. There are translations of the Qur'an into other languages, English for example (Bell 1937; Hilali and Kan 1983; Shakir 1999), but the sense of authenticity associated with the divine original in Classical Arabic is very strong. Another reason why the faithful consider the translation of scriptures problematic is to do with ambiguity. Where the original text is clear and explicit, the same contents can be expressed in another language, but where the original is vague and obscure, it is difficult to reproduce the same vagueness and obscurity in translation, thus opening the floodgates to confusion and misinterpretation. This may be intended, too. Martin Luther, a committed anti-Muslim, for example, explained how to stand up to enemies and blasphemers. As he made clear in his 'Military Sermon Against the Turks' (1529), he was in favour of reading the Qur'an and 'diligently working with it, demonstrating their law to be false and unsubstantiated' (*WA* 53: 284). To portray Muhammad as an enemy of Christianity, Luther advocated a text-critical approach, but not knowing Arabic, he needed a translation. If, however, a holy book in translation is not genuine in the first place, interpretations of a translation can never refute it.

Such are the advantages of entrusting one's creed to writing. The definitive text that allows for no deviation shields a doctrine against distortion, but also against adaptation. D'Avray (2010: 102f.) argues that, because of writing, there is little conversion between Judaism and Islam in either direction, for when values and basic ontological concepts are fixed in written formulations, they are not given up without difficulty. Logocentrism does not easily dissociate form and meaning, and its adherents may actually favour maintaining the form over understanding the meaning, thus giving preference to the symbolic over the instrumental function of language. The Greek Orthodox Church uses Greek, no matter where, and no matter whether the congregation can understand the sermon or read the holy book. Understanding is not everything in religion (Woods 2004: 13). It also must satisfy a desire for identity, expressed in ceremony and ritual, and the mysterious, which may well lie behind the veil of an antiquated and somewhat cryptic language. In religious life the spiritual dimension of language looms large (Fishman 1991: 360).

The promotion of plain language and translation is focussed on the instrumental function of language. The purpose is that common people are able to read and understand the scriptures, but that hardly means that anything goes. The association of a language with sacred texts casts a spell on it that serves the symbolic function. This function is exploited by the institutions that represent the religion to secure their privileged position as custodians of the true doctrine. Once a new translation has been completed, it quickly exhibits the same tendency towards ossification that motivated its drafting in the first place. KJV (King James Version) Onlyism is a case in point. The cherished language of the King James Version is 400 years old, and much of what was fresh and inspiring at the time is now antiquated, putting many young people off. Yet, the KJV Only Movement crusades against all attempts at modernization, which are denigrated as undermining the true doctrine. Since there can be only one authentic version, it is sometimes forgotten that it is a translation. A Midwestern preacher, according to an apocryphal story, is reported to have said, 'If the King James Bible was good enough for the apostle Paul, it is good enough for me' (Jeffrey 1996: XV).

The idea of translation is that the message is in the text and can be extracted without loss and put into another container, that is, a modernized or different language. Is it, then, immaterial in which language a doctrine is expressed? Hardly. For illustration, consider the Lol Cat Bible version of John 1,1: 'In teh beginz is teh meow, and teh meow sez "Oh hai Ceiling Cat" and teh meow iz teh Ceiling Cat. Teh meow an teh Ceiling Cat iz teh bests frenz in teh begins'.[7] This is very up-to-date and may have a certain appeal for the young generation who will have to carry the tradition further. But even devoted modernizers may question whether no barriers at all between popular culture and religion should be upheld. What Martin Luther, when he rewrote the Bible in the vernacular, was to the 'Papists' – whom, in his equally entertaining and enlightening 'Open letter on translating' (153a), he called 'knotheads who stare at words like cows at a new gate' – the authors of the Lol Cat Bible may be to the admirers of the King James Version today. If the content were all that counted and we could be persuaded that the content of the Lol Cat version of John 1,1 is exactly the same as that of the others, nothing should be amiss, but this is not so. As in other communication domains, the instrumental and the symbolic functions of language must be weighed against each other. In the course of time, as words and grammatical constructions fall out of fashion, written language, especially as the garb of a holy doctrine, gradually moves from the instrumental to the symbolic. Differences in linguistic culture manifest themselves in the kind of balance that is struck between the two. Where the symbolic is given prominence and the formal, ornate and/or archaic language of scriptures – a sacred language, a classical language or a foreign language – serves as a model for writing beyond the sphere of religious life, religion works as a cause or contributing factor to diglossia, as discussed in Chapter 2. In this sense the distance between the vernacular and the language of scriptures is indicative of social relationships and structures. A marked difference between these varieties helps to screen a religion's officials from the laity, whereas vernacularization is less hierarchical and more inclusive.

SCHOOLING: THE ABC OF WRITING

Language is a natural faculty, writing an artefact. That is the reason why children acquire language, but not writing, without guidance. The difficult art of writing requires skills that must be taught, memorized and laboriously practised. The place to do this is the school. The school is the institution that most obviously depends on writing and serves its dissemination. No writing, no school; no school, no writing. These equations are basically valid. It is not just that reading and writing are typically taught at school and that written language is learned language; much of what happens at school presupposes written text and the written mode of communication. Schools are agents of social and cultural reproduction with their own linguistic codes that are socially constructed and beyond the control of the individual.

Scribes are known to have introduced apprentices to their craft, but it is conspicuous that the school appeared early on in all literate civilizations, often connected to a temple. For writing to be useful to the community, conventions must be established, individual variation curtailed, norms set and upheld. Collective instruction following a curriculum is a more efficient way to achieve this than private tutoring. Already in antiquity the school became – and still is – the institution that most explicitly exercises authority over the written language by controlling its transmission from one generation to the next.

At the beginning of submitting language to systematic teaching stood word lists, the paradigmatic case of decontextualized language. These lists were the foundation of lexicography (Civil 1995), the science of words. In China, lexicography began with lists of characters, and characters – rather than words – are still the basic units of dictionaries. Dictionaries provide entries for lexical items. A lexical item is a word contained in a dictionary. Many more refined and less circular definitions of the 'orthographic word' as distinct from the 'phonological word' and the 'abstract lexeme' have been proposed, but it remains difficult if not impossible to define 'word' without reference to writing. The word stands at the beginning of grammatical scholarship, which was, as the word itself says, exclusively concerned with written language. *Grammatike*, combining the Greek words *grammata* 'letters' and *techne* 'art', was the art of knowing letters. These beginnings of the systematic study of language left a lasting imprint which, as Linell (2005) has shown, still informs modern linguistics. The word, the sentence and even the phoneme are analytic concepts derived from the discrete segments of writing, not vice versa. The conceptualization of writing as a representation of speech is therefore highly problematic (Harris 1980, 2000). Teaching writing in the school resulted in a changed attitude to language, which became an object of study and regulation. Neither of these concepts were in the first instance developed for and applied to speech.

Under conditions of restricted literacy, a wide divide between spoken and written language was taken for granted. Speech and writing were two modes of communication involving varieties or languages that were both grammatically and stylistically quite separate from each other. It was only when literacy was disseminated to wider sections of the population that the relationship between speech and writing became an issue. In medieval Europe the *ad litteras* reform during the reign of Charlemagne aimed at unifying spoken and written language, as the widening gap between them was perceived as a problem. It was eventually reduced, less by enforcing a uniform standard for pronouncing Latin than by dethroning Latin as the only written language and transforming *lingua illiterata* (Blanche-Benveniste 1994), that is, Romance, Germanic and Slavonic vernaculars, into written languages in their own right. Literacy in these emerging 'national' languages was bolstered by the Reformation movement that wrested the monopoly of the interpretation of Christian scriptures from the Catholic clergy. 'Write as you speak', a maxim that can be traced back to antiquity, became an increasingly important principle for writing instruction (Müller 1990). Although it unrealistically denies the speech/writing distinction, generations of teachers have repeated it to their pupils. It never meant that their writing should be as elliptical, situation-bound and variable as their speech. The implication is that if you cannot 'write as you speak', something must be wrong with your speech. Universal education on the basis of this maxim resulted in a conceptual reduction of the distance between speech and writing with some notable consequences. Mass literacy through schooling led to the disappearance of diglossia from most European speech communities, although the dichotomy of speech and writing continues to be expressed in stylistic differences.

In other parts of the world where universal education was realized later, the split between spoken and written language remained. In today's world – the 1953 UNESCO declaration recommending mother tongue literacy notwithstanding – literacy education in the language of the nation state often means learning to read and write in a second or foreign language. To what extent progress in the promotion of literacy depends on the language of instruction is still a matter of controversy, as is whether the writing system is a significant variable. To some extent this is so because definitions of literacy are shifting with changing socioeconomic needs and technical innovations, and because the range of varieties considered to be varieties of a given language is variable. There is, however, wide agreement that the crucial variable is the effectiveness of the educational system. Mastering the written language is a difficult task which is best executed by the institution that at the same time administers the written language: the school.

Since the time of the French Revolution, schools have been charged with establishing the national language and spreading the national language ideology (Schiffman 1996). As a result, the demands of multilingual education are often at variance with the state-sponsored educational system. However, because of the nationalization of languages in the modern nation state and their privileged position in the school system, the language of literacy training became a political issue. Minority speech communities aspired to gain for their languages the prestige that comes with a written standard and started in many industrialized countries to lobby for the inclusion of their languages in the school curriculum. Fuelled by the growing awareness of the importance of minority protection, such movements have in recent decades met with a measure of success, leading to a highly complex situation of multiple and multilingual literacies in modern societies which has attracted scholarly attention of late (Martin-Jones and Jones 2000; Kalantzis and Cope 2000; Daswani 2001; Cook and Bassetti 2005).

The prevailing view sees the establishment of a single national language with a unified written standard as facilitating universal literacy, and compulsory education as an instrument of nation building, for, rather than the general principles of writing and written language, pupils are taught the rules of spelling the national language, which do not allow for deviation. Like a catechism, a primer embodies a conventional standard which, however, is presented to the acolytes not as a preferred option, but as carved in stone for eternity. Pedagogical experiments with optionality of spellings are of very recent origin (Sebba 2007: 152). The very purpose of a primer is to impart discipline, in language and in life. Spelling rules are among the first strict norms to which children are collectively introduced. The ABC is the foundation on which the rest of school education is built, its mastery often having been portrayed not as just a technical skill, but as a moral prerequisite of a complete human being and member of society. Advertising the national spelling bee in Hawai'i, Sherie Char aptly summarizes the folk idea: 'Spelling is a fundamental skill students learn at an early age. It is the basic foundation in schools, but also an essential part in life. Without letters, we wouldn't have words. Without words, we wouldn't have language. Without language, we wouldn't be able to communicate.' She then quotes a competition official with the following words: 'The preservation of the discipline of spelling keeps alive our own concepts of what it is to be a human being.'[8]

The ideological significance attributed to spelling competence varies across nations, as do literacy rates. Comparing literacy rates internationally is notoriously difficult (Guérin-Pace and Blum 1999), but there is little doubt that Europe, where the national language ideology was first implemented, led the way. Today, however, the monolingual model of literacy is called into question by developments that, on one hand, favour English as a supplementary universal written language in many non-English-speaking countries, and, on the other, allow minority languages to make inroads into the domains of writing. The question of whether the diversification of literacy will help achieve the goal of eradicating illiteracy or whether it will compromise the alleged economic advantages of having one written standard language continues to be discussed by academics and politicians, while the complementary developments of globalization of markets and (re-)localization of cultures unfold.

CONCLUSION

The three institutional domains of language use considered in this chapter share a number of features in common that derive from their reliance on written language. They are characterized by a defining book: legal code, scripture, primer;

an authority affirmed and enforced by its officials: lawyers, priests, teachers;

a division of social roles: custodians vs laypersons (clients, followers, pupils);

an ideology that essentializes the conventional;

the notion that language can be regulated and change arrested;

self-reproducing institutional path dependence[9] and linguistic conservatism.

The language that is indexical of each of the three institutions is deliberately modulated by their lettered representatives to suit their purposes, based on the illusory notion that change can be arrested. If legal codes, scriptures and primers are regularly adapted to vernacular usage, change is evident, although the relationship between speech and writing is preserved, within a certain range of variation. If, on the other hand, the immutability of these texts and their underlying rules is insisted upon, the relationship between speech and writing, spoken and written language, changes, slowly but surely. The institutions considered here are constitutive of the society of letters in the sense of a delimited and recognizable community that sets its own standards. This is made possible by the medium of writing, which allows it to accumulate a body of literature and fix the rules for its conservation and transmission. The institutional structure of the society of letters suggests and secures a measure of stability of the written language that, through various literacy practices such as reading aloud, recitation, learning lessons, and spelling pronunciations, also affects the spoken language. Yet, the relationship between spoken and written language cannot be fixed, being as it is subject to the dynamics not just of language but of social evolution, too.

Universal education has disseminated writing widely, but at the same time increased the division of labour in society, fostering new genres and professionals who control them. To the three paradigmatic cases discussed in this chapter others could be added, such as advertising copy, medical reports, newspaper articles and research papers (see, e.g., Biber and Conrad 2009, Chapter 5). I chose the three examples for their clear connection with an institution. For it is to institutions we must refer in order to explain the variation in written style. In sociolinguistics, the heterogeneity of speech styles has been variously explained by different amounts of attention paid by speakers to their own speech (Labov 1994: 157f.), audience design theory which argues that speakers adjust to their audience (Bell 2001), and accommodation theory which explains style-shifting as a result of speakers' accommodating each other (Giles and Coupland 1991). These theories do not apply to the stylistic heterogeneity in writing. Although some acts of writing are more spontaneous than others, and spontaneous vs formal can thus be considered a dimension of stylistic variation in writing, as in speech, raising the attention level does not suffice to produce scriptures or legal literature. What is more, in their writing, court of law, church and school do not accommodate to their audience, i.e. readership, but expect the reader to accommodate – with the help of professional mediators. The interest of the mediators is twofold: (1) to mediate, and (2) to secure their own existence – that is, to make sure that mediation is necessary. In this way the increased division of labour made possible by writing creates communication gaps in society that the custodians of writing must bridge.

QUESTIONS FOR DISCUSSION

1 'Negative pregnant' means 'a denial of an allegation in which a person actually admits more than she/he denies by denying only part of the alleged fact'.
   Think of an example and discuss the merits and disadvantages of defined terms in legalese.
2 What is 'the problem of competing authorities' and why is it a problem?
3 Discuss the pros and cons of modernizing scriptures.
4 What, in your opinion, is at the root of the idea that 'The preservation of the discipline of spelling keeps alive our own concepts of what it is to be a human being'? How could spelling acquire such importance in a society?

6 Writing reform

To reform means to shatter one form and to create another, but the two sides of this act are not always equally intended nor equally successful. (George Santayana)

WRITING AS A PUBLIC GOOD

In the foregoing chapters it has become clear that writing is an indispensable form of communication in contemporary society, embedded in various institutions and replete with social meaning. We have also seen that certain officials act as mediators between the institutions they represent and the general public, driven, partly at least, by self-interest. Command of the written language, rather than being a mere technical skill, has always been and continues to be a marker of social distinction. Written language is an attribute of power, writing potentially a means of empowerment. Whose language functions as national language, official language, recognized minority language, etc., are political questions that require speech communities to make choices. 'National', 'official', 'recognized minority', etc., are modern categories that did not exist in earlier times when writing was less regulated than it became, first in the nation state and even more so in industrial society. Until the advent of general education, writing was for specialists, on the one hand, and, on the other, a private matter that allowed for much arbitrary variation. In Renaissance England, for example, English spelling 'was nothing short of chaotic' (Marshall 2011: 115), and much the same can be said of other countries and languages. Even at the threshold of modernity, Goethe still spelt the same words in various ways (*Goethe-Wörterbuch* n.d.), and no one would have thought less of him for that. The industrial age, however, brought demands for stricter regimentation, conformity and standardization, turning the written language into a *public good*, that is, a means of communication that came to be recognized as a prerequisite for success in collective endeavours, notably endeavours of the nation state.

Public goods – think of clean air or the rivers of a land – belong to no one but everyone is free to partake in them. Another crucial characteristic of public goods is that, in contradistinction to marketable commodities, using them does not reduce their availability and utility for others. On the contrary, the utility of public goods that have the form of networks increases with every user – think of telecommunications or the Internet.[1] Public goods are thus distinguished from private goods by two principal characteristics, non-exclusion and non-rivalry. However, as the example of telecommunication networks illustrates, public goods do not necessarily come for free, which raises the question of who should provide them, look after them, and finance them. The theory of public goods assumes that government intervention is required to supply goods characterized by collective benefits. Written language can be conceptualized as a public good, since its use is not consumption of exhaustible supplies, but, rather, increasing the number of users also increases its utility (Coulmas 2009). The network property of public goods favours standardization, and may outweigh intrinsic properties of the object in question. For example, the Qwerty keyboard of conventional typewriters had an effect on the design of orthographies for African languages. Deviation from and augmentation of the Qwerty layout, for instance for clicks and other non-roman letters, would be desirable in terms of linguistic fit, but the network of typists would be much smaller and the hardware – typewriters equipped with non-roman letters – would be more expensive. New orthographies for African languages were, therefore, often designed to make do with character sets represented on English or French typewriters. William Smalley, a missionary-linguist who was actively involved in designing writing systems, remarked (perhaps with his own work in mind, one wonders): 'Along with cultural imperialism it is easy to fall victim to a mechanical imperialism. The limitations of a typewriter keyboard sometimes bear more weight in the development of a writing system than do the phonemes of a language' (Smalley 1963: 14). Typewriters may be found only in museums now, but that does not invalidate the general point that technologies impose restrictions on writing. Not too long ago, prior to the spread of Unicode, when ASCII dominated cyber communication, scholars whose names included non-ASCII letters, such as German umlauts <ä, ö, ü> or barred Polish l <ł> changed the spelling of their names to avoid not being quoted and found on the Internet. The Qwerty layout may not be optimal for many African languages, and the ASCII code was clearly insufficient for the spelling of many names, but advantageous network properties persuaded speakers of African languages and people with non-ASCII names to submit to the limitations of these devices. With fonts for hundreds of languages, including ancient languages that were never printed mechanically when they were used by a community, limitations of this kind seem a matter of the past. However, present writing technology more likely than not has its own constraints, limiting our hands and our minds in ways of which we may not be aware.

However that may be, a written language has network properties and is a prototypical public good. Teaching one standard variety rather than local dialects creates a bigger, more unified community and thus a bigger market for printers and publishers and, not least, readers. The formation of a modern standard language is a long process whose beginnings, in Europe, go back to the Renaissance (cf., e.g., Yates 1983, for Italian; François 1959, for French; Fisher 1977, for English). It was closely intertwined with the emergence of nation states as the dominant form of political organization and reinforced by the industrial revolution. As literary languages became emblems of nations and media of instruction for educating a populace able to fulfil the requirements of mass production – uniformity, reliability and replication – national governments tightened their grip on them, as providers and custodians of this public good. In the industrial age, 'public good' meant that its use, exploitation and adaptation to changing circumstances could no longer be left to spontaneous change and 'natural' evolution, as used to be the case for centuries when writing conventions changed gradually without any grand plan. There were national differences, to be sure. While the Italians had a language academy, the Accademia della Crusca, long before a unified Italian nation state, and the French established an academy charged with regulating the language to suit the needs of the state bureaucracy, no such institution was founded in Britain. But these are details. The general development in Renaissance Europe is that of hegemonic languages of nation states with literacy education and written documents, especially monolingual dictionaries, as their underpinning. With the *Vocabolario della Crusca* (1612) and the *Dictionnaire de l'Académie* (1694), Italy and France were in the vanguard, but Samuel Johnson's dictionary (1755) and Noah Webster's (1806) also became national monuments, as did the *Deutsches Wörterbuch*, begun in 1838 by Jacob and Wilhelm Grimm, but completed only 123 years later.

The written language thus became an object of political designs in various ways, and public finances were made available, for instance by paying for national academies and covering the cost of mother tongue education, precisely because the national languages were recognized as

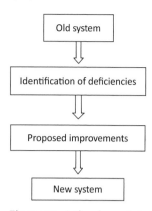

Figure 6.1 A simple model of decision making for writing reform

public goods that effect collective benefits. From the point of view of the powers that be, writing is constitutive of what a language proper is: *la langue cultivée*, a learned, normalized language governed by conventions and rules, often arbitrary, rather than unguided *use*. There is no language policy and no language planning without writing. The instrumental and symbolic functions of writing have always tempted the powerful to try to control it, purportedly in the best interest of the people. The general idea is that regulation is necessary to protect users from negative effects of change. Synchronic heterogeneity in the form of deviations from the norm, and diachronic variation, in the form of shifts in the mapping relationship between speech and writing, are prone to upset the system to the detriment of its users. Spelling as a self-regulating system does not guarantee a degree of uniformity of output high enough for the needs of industrial society. These needs are rarely mentioned explicitly as motivating writing reforms; other values such as the rationality, dignity, beauty and distinctness of a system are invoked as well. Again it is both instrumental and symbolic functions of language that come to bear, rather than practical utility alone. For this and other reasons, writing reforms tend to have political undertones and often turn out to be highly controversial – for writing reforms involve the speech community and are not easily carried out by decree: acceptance is crucial. These reforms embody claims to ownership and authority over a society's language and as such are an interesting case of public choice. An extremely simple model of the decision-making process underlying any writing reform can be depicted as in Fig. 6.1.

It is a simple model and also a simplistic one, for, as we shall see, each box represents a complex combination of several influences. For instance, considering the fact that in pre-modern times few people could ever get worked up about spelling, the emotions that spelling reform proposals often arouse in our age are quite remarkable, suggesting that the mass distribution of the written word as a public good through general education has imbued spelling with ideological contents of modernity, notably the permeation of standards in many spheres of life. Rather than a mere technical skill, spelling in nineteenth- and twentieth-century schools was framed in terms of character formation, morality and national pride and distinction. Noah Webster's *American Spelling Book*, which included a moral catechism and a patriotic catechism, is paradigmatic, though hardly the only example (Grillo 1989).

The written language can be normalized; a standard can be defined and declared valid. However, an alphabetic writing system, unlike, for example, Chinese characters, suggests a close mapping relationship between speech and writing; writing reform will be necessary at certain intervals lest this mapping relationship become ever more intricate, for even in fully literate societies people do not speak as they write, or pronounce as they spell. Since writing is an artefact, every writing system could always be better than it is. As long as writing is writing of a particular language, there will be no writing system refined to perfection. As a tool developed at a given point in history for certain purposes, every writing system will always be subject to demands for its improvement in terms of linguistic fit, learnability or political correctness.

The uses of writing in modern societies are intimately linked with storing, retrieving and securing access to information in a standardized form that, moreover, ensures continuity. Writing reforms, therefore, need official sanction. The general motivation for such reforms is to secure the functionality of the system by simplifying its rules and thus to facilitate the task of children becoming literate. Because written language is associated with institutions such as school, the church and courts of law, it has almost always proven difficult to limit the discussion to linguistic aspects in the narrow sense. Culture is an important background aspect which interacts with political, economic and social determinants of language regulation (Fodor and Hagège 1983–90).

LINGUISTIC ASPECTS OF WRITING REFORMS

Since writing is fixed, while language is in flux, the relationship between the two is subject to distortion over time. As a general rule, the smaller the basic operational unit of the writing system, the sooner inconsistencies between writing and speech will appear. A morphemic writing system will require adjustments at greater intervals than one that maps onto sound segments, because sound change is more rapid than morphological change. With a few exceptions, writing systems were not deliberately designed, but evolved more or less spontaneously. Therefore, and because of the historicity of language, all writing systems constitute suboptimal solutions to the problem of establishing relationships between graphical and linguistic units.

Ever since the Carolingian reforms in the Middle Ages, which were intended to check the corruption of Latin by making people throughout the Empire pronounce it *ad litteras*, spelling reforms have been designed to reduce the gap between pronunciation and orthography. In modern times, however, adjustments have generally been in the opposite direction, bringing the spelling in line with pronunciation. Considering the phonetic variation of any sizeable language, this is easier said than done. A more moderate aim is to make phoneme–grapheme relations more consistent. Uniformity, transparency and simplicity are common aims of spelling reforms, as for example in the Dutch (van der Sijs 2004), German (Eroms and Munske 1997), French (AIROÉ 2000) and Spanish (Del Valle and Villa 2012) orthography reforms of 1995, 1996, 2000 and 2010, respectively. All of these reforms claim to simplify the spelling rules. Since many rules are quite abstract and/or complicated, and since there are always reasons to retain irregular spellings, the four reforms include, in addition to a set of rules, long word lists of approved spellings. These lists suggest that regularity that can be captured by a simple set of rules is hard to achieve.

The said reforms do not alter any basic design features of the orthographies in question, pertaining to accent marks, word separation, the use of capital letters, and the integration of loan words, as well as some other lesser problems. In all four cases international institutional efforts were made to realize the reform, yet they met with major resistance from defenders of the old norms. As a result, rival conventions coexist. Purists are disturbed by this state of affairs, but many readers, writers and publishers do not seem to be concerned. This highlights one of the most interesting questions about spelling reforms in our day. Has the mastering of spelling rules in the age of spell-checker software become less important? Does the rigid notion of one and only one correct spelling eventually reveal its true nature as a product of industrial society, while major European standard languages enter into a phase of de-standardization characteristic of post-industrial society? Spellcheckers for English, French and Spanish, for example, come in more than a dozen variants each. For a relatively short period of time, sanctioned orthographies were testimony to the authority of nation states over language use. In industrial society, the principal agent of executing this authority was compulsory education, in which fixed orthographic norms were a key element of the curriculum, instilling in the pupils a sense of exactitude and uniformity. Complaints in the Western media about increasingly lenient high school teachers, on one hand, and college students who can't spell, on the other, suggest that this period may be on the wane and that state authority over language is giving way to market forces. To answer the question of whether this is the case, more research is needed about how speech communities deal with variation in writing and with computer-mediated text production.

Advocates of writing reform invariably cite purely objective reasons to argue their case for the benefit of the community concerned. Yet they usually receive large numbers of angry comments from a public that is not easily convinced of this benefit. This is typical of public choice in government, where interventions are presented as being grounded in objective criteria and invariably billed as 'only for your own good'. Recurrent criteria for the evaluation of writing systems are transparency, regularity and simplicity. For example, Italian children spell better than their English-speaking peers, which has been attributed to the Italian spelling system being more transparent than the English one (Cossu 1999). However, the influence of other factors, such as teaching methods and social attitudes to literacy, are rarely controlled for. Findings such as the fact that the English reading ability of Singaporean children is superior to that of Irish and American children (Elley 1993) cannot be explained on linguistic grounds. A well-known project to deal with the intricacies of English spelling was the Initial Teaching Alphabet (ITA) developed by Sir James Pitman (Pitman and St John 1969). ITA is more or less phonemic and much more transparent than English spelling. In the 1960s it was tested in British schools and proved to be helpful for pupils with severe reading disabilities, but in spite of extensive research no hard evidence has been produced to demonstrate that children learn more effectively with ITA than with the conventional English orthography. Similarly, nothing indicates that American spelling is learnt more easily than British spelling, although the former is supposedly more regular and simpler.

Linguistic reasons for writing and spelling reforms are multifarious and cogent. In some measure, improvements of transparency, inner logic and linguistic motivation are always possible. Whether or not such improvements have any effect on a script's learnability and usability is a different matter. So far, compelling evidence that design features of writing systems help or hinder the process of becoming literate has been elusive. In regard to literacy, linguistic motivations for writing reform, therefore, seem to be of secondary importance at best. Sebba (2007) has argued that linguistic orthography studies tend to treat orthography as a neutral structure and fail to recognize adequately its sociocultural nature, which, however, should be reckoned with in any writing reform. He therefore advocates the notion of 'orthography as practice', subject to the formative influence of institutions, traditions and attitudes.

SOCIAL ASPECTS OF WRITING REFORMS

A principal motivation of writing reforms is to make the acquisition of literacy easier and thus provide for wider access to education. A major reform undertaken in the fifteenth century by King Sejong the Great in Korea is an early example. Korean used to be written with Chinese characters, which were not only very numerous but also ill suited to the Korean language (Shin, Lee and Lee 1990; Kim-Renaud 1997). The king, therefore, ordered a new, purely phonetic writing system to be drawn up which would be: (1) more suitable for Korean, and (2) easier to learn than the Chinese one. This task was accomplished admirably. The new system, known nowadays as *Han'gŭl*, was very simple, consisting of only twenty-eight letters with unequivocal phonetic interpretations, of which twenty-four are in use today. While Chinese literacy was the privilege of a small elite, the new system proved to be easy to learn – too easy for its critics, who disparagingly called it *ach'imgŭl* ('morning letters') or *amk'ŭl* ('women's letters'), implying that the new alphabet could be learnt in one morning and even by women. This was in stark contrast with the many years of study that full literacy in Chinese required. Those who had undertaken this task perceived the new phonetic script as a threat to their intellectual authority and privileged position in society, an attitude that commonly accompanies writing reforms that involve a shift from one system to another (Fishman 1988: 280).

Chinese writing, too, has been the subject of various reforms. After the first Opium War (1840–3) a language movement that attributed China's weakness and backwardness to its literary culture gained momentum (Chen 1996). Intellectuals argued that Chinese characters were a major impediment to mass literacy and set out to investigate alternatives to the traditional script. In the twentieth century, these efforts were continued in recognition of the importance of education for empowering the masses. During the first decades of the century various schemes for the Romanization of Chinese were developed, such as the 'National Phonetic Alphabet' (*Zhuyin Zimu*) promulgated in 1918, the 'National Language Romanization' (*Gwoyeu Romatzyh*) promulgated in 1928, and the 'Latinized New Writing System' (*Latinxua Sin Wenz*), published in 1929 in the Soviet Union. The authors of these schemes and Chinese government officials agreed that a more manageable written language was needed.

After the founding of the People's Republic of China (PRC) in 1949, writing reform remained a government priority, with Chairman Mao himself getting involved in the discussion (DeFrancis 1950). Initially the government seemed committed to replacing Chinese characters with a Latin orthography. To this end, *Pinyin*, based on 'common speech', or *Putonghua*, which is the pronunciation of Beijing, was developed by the Committee for Writing System Reform of China. However, when it was promulgated by the government in 1958 it was no longer intended to replace characters, but to perform auxiliary functions, such as indicating the pronunciation of characters.

A second reform serving the same superordinate purpose of facilitating the acquisition of literacy was pursued at the same time: character simplification (Coulmas 1983). A first list of simplified characters in common use was drafted in 1956, and after a long process of deliberation and improvement the government published a list of 1,754 simplified characters in 1964. A second character simplification scheme was promulgated in 1977, although in the face of confusion and opposition this was rescinded in 1986. In the end only the 1956 reform was implemented and had a lasting effect on the written language (Zhao and Baldauf, Jr 2011)

Character simplification consists essentially of standardizing cursive forms and reducing the number of constituent strokes. The rationale underlying this approach is that fewer strokes mean less work in both the learning and writing of characters. The potential risks are that simplified characters will be less distinct and more difficult to identify with historically earlier forms. These are valid concerns making it easy for opponents to resist the reform. Taiwan refused to join the reform for other reasons, stressing its autonomy and proving itself as the bearer of Chinese tradition. For many years no innovation that came from the PRC was acceptable in Taiwan, certainly not one that would amount to recognizing the PRC's authority over something so symbolically charged as the Chinese writing system. As a result, simplified and unabbreviated characters are now used concurrently in the Chinese-speaking world, exemplifying a common pattern of written language use in the wake of many writing reforms. Proponents and opponents, often split along lines of political inclinations between conservatives and progressives, both rely on their own reputable experts to support their position. This shows how difficult it is to keep practical and symbolic aspects of writing reforms apart, and that writing reforms are hard to implement in the absence of complete control over the territory and/or the population concerned.

It seems to stand to reason that standardizing Chinese characters, reducing their graphical complexity and their number, would be conducive to mass literacy, but this is hard to prove. The reason is that the success of literacy education depends on many variables, and real-life conditions outside educational laboratories are highly complex. Literacy in the PRC has been lower than in Taiwan for decades and still lags behind, but this does not imply anything about the suitability of unabbreviated characters for literacy education. It does not even justify the conclusion that the effects of the PRC's writing reform are negligible. What we can learn from the Chinese case is that relationships between structural properties of writing systems and literacy levels are hard to substantiate. As Taylor and Taylor (1995), among others, have argued, Chinese characters do not in and of themselves present an obstacle to mass literacy. There may nevertheless be good reasons for periodic writing reforms, such as harmonizing standard and current usage as well as eliminating inconsistencies.

The fact that the PRC trailed Taiwan in literacy rates even though the latter uses more complex characters can be attributed to social factors such as the more advanced degree of urbanization in Taiwan. This assumption is also supported by the Japanese experience. Although Japanese educators had toyed with Romanization since Japan entered the period of industrialization late in the nineteenth century, they never abandoned the traditional mixed system of Chinese characters and the Japanese-developed syllabic kana. Yet, under the American occupation, the United States Education Mission of 1946 recommended that Japan consider adopting a Romanized script instead. Some experiments were carried out, but they came to nothing (Unger 1996), which evidently did not hinder Japan in achieving a very high degree of literacy and climbing to the top of international scholastic achievement tests. These observations about Chinese character-based writing systems are of more general interest, as they call into question the causal relationship that has often been assumed to hold between writing system and literacy, that is, between the complexity of the system and the spread of literacy in society. Notably, low literacy rates in the USA and other Anglophone countries have been blamed on the intricacies of English spelling (Bell 2004), which the Simplified Spelling Society calls 'a serious obstacle to education'.[2] How serious – if at all – is a matter of controversy. Conclusive evidence of negative effects of complex writing systems on educational achievement has proved difficult to establish. It is possible that, although writing systems differ in complexity, this difference is not a crucial predictor of how quickly and well children learn to read, let alone social literacy levels, but is outweighed by other variables, such as school curriculum, teaching methods, pupils' language background, enforcement of compulsory education, social attitudes towards literacy, etc. Since these factors can only be controlled under laboratory conditions, it is virtually impossible to determine the effects of writing reforms on literacy.

POLITICAL ASPECTS OF WRITING REFORM

Writing reform does not necessarily carry a political direction, but is often associated with and motivated by political goals. The form of the written language is a marker of identity which lends itself easily to political instrumentalization. A well-known example is the Turkish language reform of the 1920s, which was part of Kemal Atatürk's nationalist modernization movement. In the event, the Arabic script used throughout the Ottoman Empire for Turkish and several other languages all over Central Asia was replaced by the Latin alphabet. Symbolically, the adoption of the Latin alphabet in 1928 indicated a reorientation of Turkey's foreign relations and the desire to strengthen economic and cultural ties with Europe. Prior to the reform, the Persian-derived alphabet of Ottoman Turkish, which had only three different vowel letters, was never seen as a problem, but in the context of the modernization discourse the paucity of vowel letters was considered deficient for Turkish. Its eight vowels were thus assigned the Latin letters <i, ü, ı, u, e, ö, a, o>. At the same time, Turkish purists campaigned for reducing the lexical dependence of Turkish on Arabic and Persian loans by creating many new words on the basis of Turkish roots to replace them. Turkish in the Latin script symbolized a cultural and political reorientation of the country, a turning away from the Ottoman past and an alignment with the European future. Regaining national self-esteem after the collapse of the Ottoman Empire was part of the political background. In Atatürk's words: 'The Turkish nation, which is well able to protect its territory and sublime independence, must also liberate its language from the yoke of foreign languages' (quoted from Lewis 2002: 42).

Similar script reforms were carried out in the orbit of the Soviet Union, first when it was founded and again when it dissolved. In Azerbaijan, for instance, the Soviet government initially – i.e. in the early 1920s – promoted literacy in the new Latin Turkic Alphabet 'to free the proletariat from the Arabic script' (Clement 2005, quoted in Hatcher

Table 6.1 *Cyrillic letters and their Roman equivalents*

Cyrillic	а	б	в	г	д	е	ж	з	и	к	Л	м	н	о	п	р	с	т	у	ф	х	ц	ч	ш	ы	ь	э	ю	я
Roman	a	b	v	g	d	e	j	z	i	c	l	m	n	o	p	r	s	t	u	f	h	ț	c	ș	â	i	ă	iu	ea

2008: 107). Under Stalin, however, the Latin script was replaced by Cyrillic, for fear that, in the wake of Atatürk's language reform, the Latin alphabet would create an unwelcome link between Turkey and Turkic minorities in the USSR. Within months of the demise of the USSR in 1991, the Azerbaijani Parliament reinstated the Latin alphabet as the official script, resisting calls from Teheran to return to the Arabic script, which is used by the large Azeri minority in Iran.

Turkmenistan underwent parallel shifts. In the post-Soviet period the Turkmens divested themselves of Cyrillic, opting instead for a Latin orthography which, by striving for one-to-one phoneme–letter correspondence, differed markedly from the Common Turkic Script promoted by Turkey. In 1993, the Turkmen National Alphabet was promulgated as a symbol of national independence and renewal. The expectation that it would be conducive to literacy was offered as an additional motivation: 'to mark every phoneme with an individual grapheme, scholars believed, would facilitate learning to read' (Clement 2008: 178).

Roman and Cyrillic are structurally identical alphabets that are easily transliterated into each other (Table 6.1). The motivation for substituting one for the other is primarily ideological rather than practical. The writing of Moldovan furnishes a good example. When the disintegration of the Soviet Union was in sight, the Moldavian Soviet Socialist Republic passed a Law in 1989 on the Functioning of Languages on the Territory of Moldova which assigned the status of official language to Moldovan, as Romanian in Cyrillic letters was known. It also stipulated that the Latin alphabet be used for the official language, thereby eliminating the visual differences between Moldovan and Romanian which had been cultivated during Soviet times in order to strengthen relations with the Cyrillic languages to the east of Moldova, especially Russian and Ukrainian. The 1994 constitution of the Republic of Moldova declared the status of Moldovan as the national language, and its written form as based on the Latin alphabet. The name of the language, i.e. 'Moldovan' vs 'Romanian', remained a bone of contention, as parts of the population consider themselves ethnic Romanians, whereas others prefer to stress their independence and 'maintain that they speak Moldovan' (Angheli 2003: 72). The replacement of Cyrillic by the Roman alphabet suggests a break with the Soviet past, but keeping a distinct name for the language indicates that unification with Romania is not desired.

Script reforms are often politically motivated and arouse political passion. To a larger extent than spelling reforms they constitute a disruption of intellectual life and a break with the past, making literature in the old script inaccessible to the non-specialist. Only where the literacy level of the general population is very low and a strong ideology, particularly nationalism, secures the reform's popularity does this not endanger successful implementation. Since both these preconditions existed in post-Ottoman Turkey, the shift from Arabic to Latin letters was accomplished without major problems. In the post-Soviet republics literacy levels were higher, and script reform schemes generally provoked more discussion and resistance.

The power behind an ideology is another decisive factor. When the Vietnamese adopted an alphabetic writing system in the late nineteenth century, they had used Chinese characters for a thousand years. But as the influence of Chinese civilization faltered under the onslaught of Western imperialism and the French established themselves in Indochina, their argument that the alphabet spelt progress and education for the masses was persuasive. Although the literacy rate in Vietnam declined under French rule (as it did in Algeria), the Vietnamese fully embraced what had come to them originally as a tool of Christian proselytism, and, inspired by anti-colonialism and nationalist policies, applied it successfully to mass literacy promotion (Lo Bianco 2000: 103). Vietnam thus became the only Confucian society to abandon the most conspicuous symbol and tool of Chinese civilization, Chinese characters. Nowadays, Chinese characters are still found in inscriptions in Vietnam, but their function is almost entirely reduced to the emblematic and decorative. Replacing a centuries-old writing system by a structurally completely different one is a rare occurrence, for cultural path dependence makes such drastic action very difficult. In Viet Nam, as in Turkey, shifting power relations, a modernization ideology that resonated with the masses and a relatively low level of the 'old' literacy combined to dislodge an old imperial system that linked the literary elite to a universal tradition and to establish a new, national literacy instead.

Because of their political embeddedness it is difficult to make generalizations about spelling reforms, their success and failure, and the extent of public support and opposition. Some reforms on a much smaller scale than the system shifts in Viet Nam and Turkey never made it beyond the drawing board, or triggered extensive debates. The most recent German spelling reform is a case in point. German spelling reformers have for a century wrestled with the problem of capitalization. Martin Luther, whose Bible translation served as the principal reference point for correct spelling from the sixteenth century, only used initial capitals for 'God', the names of some prophets and the sentence-initial word. In the course of time this rather simple though clearly not linguistically motivated convention gave way to an abundance of capital letters in German texts that on several occasions triggered calls for reform. Defenders of the practice of capitalizing the initial letters of nouns emphasize that majuscules facilitate parsing. However, the advantages, if any, for the reader are easily outweighed by the disadvantages for the writer, given that 'a word spelt with an initial capital' is the most common dictionary definition of what a German noun is. (Thus, in order to decide whether to spell a word with an upper-case initial letter you have to know whether it is a noun, which depends on whether it is spelt with an upper-case initial.) Yet the drive for reform gained momentum, not least because of an increase in the numbers of pupils diagnosed with dyslexia and other reading disorders.

The most recent reform, the first since the publication of the *Duden* dictionary at the beginning of the twentieth century, was a national and, indeed, an international affair from the start, since authority over language is considered a matter of national sovereignty. In the early 1980s, a commission was established that included West German, East German, Swiss and Austrian representatives who, presumably, also kept German-speaking minorities in Denmark, Belgium, France and Italy in the back of their minds. Friends and foes of capital letters marshalled their troops – linguists, psychologists, educators – and after about ten years of deliberation the mountain laboured and brought forth the mouse of a reform proposal for *gemäßigte Kleinschreibung* (moderate abolition of capital letters) (Coulmas 1998). It dealt with irregularities in five areas: grapheme–phoneme correspondence; capitalization; the spelling of compounds; hyphenation and word division at the end of a line; and punctuation. Some anachronistic spellings were eliminated and some rules simplified, but overall changes were moderate and would not change written German out of recognition. However, no sooner was the proposal made public in 1995 than a storm of protest erupted which, in Germany, led to a major legal wrangle right up to the Bundesverfassungsgericht (Federal Constitutional Court), the country's highest court (Johnson 2003). The Court ruled that the reform was too limited to threaten any constitutional rights and could thus be implemented. But that was not the end of the matter. In one of West Germany's federal states, Schleswig-Holstein, the reform was defeated in a referendum, 56.4 per cent to 29.1 per cent. Since Germany has no federal

Table 6.2 *German spelling, old and new, some examples*

Old spelling (1901)	New spelling (2006)	Meaning
heute abend	heute Abend	tonight
außer acht lassen	außer Acht lassen	to ignore
in bezug auf	in Bezug auf	with reference to
ebensogut	ebenso gut	as well
groß geschrieben	großgeschrieben	capitalized
Midlife-crisis	Midlifecrisis	midlife crisis
Im nachhinein	Im Nachhinein	after the fact
Paragraph	Paragraph/Paragraf	paragraph
Rolladen	Rollladen	shutters
4zeilig	4-zeilig	Four-line

ministry of education, there is no authority that could resolve the ensuing impasse. The highest court had ruled, textbooks had been printed
in the reformed spelling, but the result of the referendum could hardly
be ignored by the cultural bureaucracy of Schleswig-Holstein. Eventually, in 2006, a compromise was achieved and a watered-down reform
was implemented. Some diehard reform critics such as the conservative
Frankfurter Allgemeine Zeitung stuck to their guns and refused to accept
the new rules, citing the highest court's ruling that allowed individuals
to continue writing according to the old rules.

The material content of the reform is trivial (see Table 6.2 for some
examples), but the commotion that accompanied it is noteworthy. For
whatever reasons, people found it worth their while to read extensively
about spelling in the newspapers, fill 'letters to the editor' columns,
assemble in PTA and many other meetings, collect signatures, write
petitions and vote in a referendum. Educators, publishers, writers,
politicians, lawyers and the general public got involved, while few
people voiced misgivings about referring the reform to the courts that
were called upon to determine its legality. The subject of the debate, the
written form of the national language, was such that many people felt
qualified to partake in it. Since no social research about the underlying
motives has been conducted, we can only speculate why the spelling
reform provoked so much zeal and fervour: esteem for the standard
language as a cultural achievement; respect for officialdom and a
rule-giving authority; an overestimation of the importance of spelling
(and, perhaps, lack of other problems). Here we see that, difficult as it
is to draw any general conclusions, writing reform has to reckon with
political realities rather than being an academic matter that can be
settled by specialists.

Involving a country's highest court as ultimate arbitrator seems to ascribe spelling an inordinate measure of importance. But why stop at national courts?! There is a reported case of a conflict about orthography in post-Soviet-era Belarusian in which supporters and opponents of a 1933 reform were pitted against each other. Supporters of the traditional – that is, pre-1933 – spelling managed to get international human rights organizations to invoke international law – the International Covenant of Civil and Political Rights – in order to challenge the Belarus media law of 1998 which prohibits the press from 'distorting the generally accepted norms of the language' (Maksymiuk 1999: 142). Since the pre-1933 spelling represents Belarus authenticity in a non-Russian, non-Soviet key, while the 1933 reform was decreed by Soviet apparatchiks and still bears that association for some traditionalists, the dispute, as in many similar cases, is quite obviously about political symbolism rather than linguistic technicalities. This does not invalidate the technicalities, but it puts the significance of linguistic arguments for and against spelling reforms into perspective.

ECONOMIC ASPECTS OF WRITING REFORM

Writing reform proposals are often motivated by economic considerations having to do with markets in a manner reminiscent of the advances of standardized spelling conventions in the wake of the spread of printing with movable type in the fifteenth and early sixteenth centuries in Europe. The printing industry has a vested interest in unifying the spelling conventions of French, German, Dutch, Portuguese, among others, across national boundaries. The economies of scale in, for example, school book publishing are very considerable, which is, presumably, why some British publishers have adopted American spelling. Printing and publishing is Britain's third-largest industry and plays a similarly important role in other countries with 'big' languages. García Delgado and Alonso's remark about the 'possibilities associated with the commercialization of products that depend centrally on language', in that case Spanish, holds for all languages with a wider reach: 'One of the first and most immediate economic dimensions of language has to do with teaching as a business activity, an area that lends itself to entrepreneurial initiatives' (quoted in Del Valle and Villa 2006: 375).

From the point of view of the printing industry, spelling conventions can thus be viewed as delimiting markets (although digital technology has made it much easier and cheaper to deal with alternative conventions). The cost-cutting imperative calls for unified spellings for

Portuguese in Portugal and Brazil, Dutch in the Netherlands and Belgium, German in German-speaking countries, etc. Ultimately, the general acceptance of one convention by all parties concerned is more important than which one it should be. Yet, on occasion, the nature of the spelling system itself is also subjected to economic assessment. Repeatedly, efficiency arguments in favour of spelling reforms have been invoked on the levels of system design and learning. These are related and lead to the common claim that a writing system is in need of reform because it is uneconomical. For example: 'Billions of dollars are lost each year through our archaic spelling, which is a prime cause of academic discouragement and failure. We throw money away trying to teach it and money away trying to use it' (Citron 1981: 181). This is a typical statement which rests on certain ideas of humanity and writing, that is, that humans are by nature thrifty (lazy) and that this human trait has determined the history of writing. These ideas have been argued most forcefully in Zipf's (1949) book, tellingly entitled *Human Behavior and the Principle of Least Effort*, and Gelb's (1963) *A Study of Writing*.[3] 'Zipf's Law' states that the relationship between a word's frequency of occurrence and its rank on a frequency scale for a given corpus is a constant, in the sense that there is a fixed proportion between a small number of high-frequency words and a large number of words with a low frequency of occurrence. This distribution, according to Zipf, testifies to the force of the Principle of Least Effort, which is at work in all human behaviour, specifically in the creation and development of tools, since the conservation of energy results in an evolutionary advantage. Gelb (1963: 72) similarly postulated 'a principle of economy' underlying the history of writing, which aims 'at the effective expression of the language by means of the smallest possible number of signs'.

Some writing systems, notably Sumerian and Akkadian Cuneiform, with which Gelb was most familiar, reduced their sign inventory over time, but the argument that this is a universal principle of evolutionary progression governing the history of writing is untenable, because inventory size interacts with other properties of writing systems that determine ease of use and learning, especially simplicity, unequivocalness and faithfulness. For example, Japanese kana are more numerous than the 26 letters of English, but learning kana is much easier and faster than learning English spelling. And while the 29-letter Finnish alphabet does not differ significantly in size from the English, learning Finnish spelling, too, is much easier than English. Why is this so? The obvious answer is that the size of the inventory of the basic signs of a writing system does not predict the degree of its complexity. Finnish orthography is very transparent and regular, both in spelling-to-sound and sound-to-spelling relationships (Lehtonen 2005: 64). English, by contrast, is opaque and multi-valued in both directions with more than 280 graphemes (26 single-letter graphemes, 153 two-letter graphemes, three-letter graphemes and a few in excess of that) and anywhere between 220 and 250 phono-graphic rules (Carney 1994). Hence English spelling must be seen as a violation of the Principle of Least Effort brought about by language contact with French, the incorporation of numerous loan words in their original spelling and the failure to correct outdated phoneme–grapheme correspondences, etc., and, therefore, should, in the eyes of some, be reformed.

However, every writing system involves both memory and combinatorial rules. The multiplicity of extant writing systems suggests that there is a great range for striking a balance between the two, some relying more on memory, others more on analysis/synthesis. In some languages, such as, for example Finnish, a few analytic rules to synthesize the correct spelling of the vast majority of all words suffice, while in other languages, such as English, it is more useful to commit the spelling of a large number of words to memory. What is more, the balance that has been found for the graphic form of a language does not necessarily stay the same. For instance, making use of a 26-letter alphabet, English has shifted ever more from analysis/synthesis to memory. Thus, even if Gelb's principle of economy has certain merits for the early history of writing, its pertinence for explaining current differences between writing systems is limited (Daniels 2008), as is its significance for planning writing reforms.

This observation suggests that either the Principle of Least Effort is not as universal as claimed, or the notion that some writing systems are measurably more economical than others is problematic. Even if writing systems could be ranked for complexity, which is by no means self-evident, there is a conspicuous lack of evidence to support the claim that the relative complexity of writing systems is a significant variable of determining mass literacy levels. Hence, on closer inspection, the argument that writing reforms are called for in order to reduce waste fails to convince.

CONCLUSIONS

Two kinds of writing reform have been discussed in this chapter: writing system reform and orthography reform. Both have various rationales, linguistic, social, political and economic, that interact in multiple ways with one another. It would be desirable to rank these factors according to their relative weight and influence on the outcome of reform schemes, but in view of the great diversity of linguistic and social starting conditions this seems hardly possible. Yet, from the cases reviewed above certain generalizations can be drawn.

1 Both language and writing evolve through time. The latter is an abstraction and an artificial model of the former which is open to deliberate intervention (reform).

2 At any given time the language system, especially the sound system, is the result of largely spontaneous and unguided change. Spontaneous adjustments affect writing systems, too, but writing conventions are fixed and subject to conscious reflection to a much higher degree than the rules of the language. They are artefacts, and every change is an artefact.

3 Writing is an artefact that, in addition to being an instrument of visual communication, lends itself easily to, and is accordingly often employed for, symbolic (emblematic) purposes.

4 Any writing reform, therefore, has instrumental and symbolic aspects.

5 Because of the artificial nature of writing as an explicit convention which to a greater or lesser extent is dependent on official sanction, instrumental considerations for reform are likely to be compromised by symbolic ones.

Linguists involved in writing reforms have invariably come to the insight that systematic and theoretically well-founded reasoning does not unreservedly prevail. Under the bottom line, ideological arguments outweigh functional ones – that is, issues of systematicity and orthographic efficiency. This is so because the writing system is the most conspicuous linguistic subsystem which non-linguists tend to take as representing the language itself, its history and symbolic value as a marker of identity. It is rare that a speech community takes no or only little interest in a writing reform, regarding it as a technicality that should be left to experts. An attempt to change it is therefore likely to become an object of discussion by various parties that claim the right to be heard and involved in the decision-making process.

Let us now return to the model in Figure 6.1, which is repeated here for convenience.

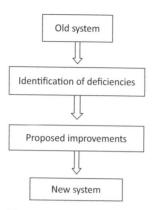

Figure 6.1 A simple model of decision making for writing reform

As we have seen, several stakeholders who try to influence the outcome are involved: experts, official institutions, private business and the general public. Since their expertise, preferences and motivations are not typically congruent, the reformed system is bound to reflect motivations and demands of the kinds addressed in this chapter, that is, linguistic, social, political and economic ones. Taking these into account, we arrive at a more complicated picture, as in Figure 6.2.

The model in Figure 6.2 suggests that the final outcome of any writing reform will be a compromise. It would be theoretically more satisfying if we could say that the model *predicts* or *implies* a compromise, but given the heterogeneity of inputs the terms *predict* and *imply* are too strong and neat. Social reality is too messy for that. 'Suggest' suggests a high degree of probability, and that is all we can say. As social artefacts and public goods, writing systems are an integral part of the social process and are, therefore, unlikely ever to be shaped on purely scientific grounds. It is certainly not, as a matter of principle, impossible that a speech community should leave the supervision and periodic updating of its writing system to specialists and accept their prescriptions without question; but it is unlikely, for two reasons.

1 The trouble starts with disagreement among experts. Recall, for instance, the description of English orthography as 'a near optimal system for the lexical representation of English words' (Chomsky and Halle 1968: 49). Noam Chomsky is the most important linguist of our time, and his views must be taken seriously; but they are of a theoretical nature that will not necessarily convince reform-minded educators who have different priorities. Reading

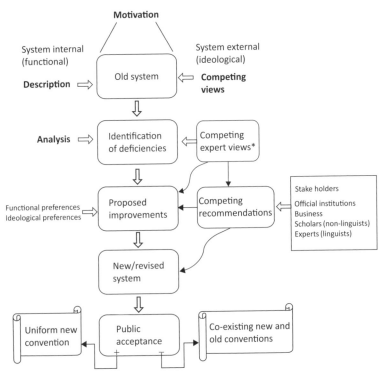

* For example, about maintaining the original spelling of loan words or nativizing them, e.g. spelling Chinese and Japanese place names with or without tone marks (Táiwān vs Taiwan) and macrons for long vowels (Tōkyō vs Tokyo), respectively.

Figure 6.2 A realistic model of decision making for writing reform

psychologists, historians and archivists, among others, have different standards and are likely to highlight different aspects describing the orthography. Even if they arrive at similar descriptions, they may emphasize in their reform recommendations different principles that are at work in the system, such as homophone differentiation or phono-graphic consistency.

2 A writing system is not just a technical software, but, as it were, a multifunctional social software subject to preferences, attitudes, emotions and political designs. Moreover, in many cases – in English, for example – the range of dialects makes it virtually impossible to find a solution satisfactory to all. New spellings are unfamiliar and, for that reason alone, found objectionable by many. In many reform proposals, doing away with unnecessary oddities – such as functionless accent marks in Greek, the curly double 's' <ß> in German, the 'tilde' <accent mark> in Spanish

words like *guión* – met with the strongest emotional resistance. For most people concerned, scientific rigour is not the ultimate criterion of spelling reforms. Emotional attachments and political sympathies interfere with the benefits of regularity and parsimony. When it comes to tradition, routine and identity, reducing the number of rules, saving some ink, some memory space or some muscle power of eye movements apparently count for little. Since writing is no longer the prerogative of an elite but a universal means of social participation, many people feel both entitled and qualified to voice their opinions about writing their language. As a result, the perpetuation of inconsistencies and the introduction of new ones seem an inevitable side-effect of writing reforms.

QUESTIONS FOR DISCUSSION

1 Noah Webster's *American Spelling Book* published around 1800 contained two appendices, a Moral Catechism and a Federal Catechism. The following Q-and-A sequence is part of the latter.

> Q. It is not unjust that all should be bound to obey a law, when all do not consent to it?
> A. Every thing is JUST in government which is NECESSARY to the PUBLIC GOOD. It is impossible to bring all men to think alike on all subjects, so that if we wait for all opinions to be alike respecting laws, we shall have no laws at all.[4]

Discuss the question of why the two catechisms would be included in a spelling book and whether the quoted sequence applies to spelling.

2 Who benefits from a standardized spelling system?

3 In 2010, the Real Academia Española (the royal Spanish language academy) issued new spelling rules for Spanish. They include the declassification of <ll> and <ch> as letters in their own right, the renaming of <y> as *ye* instead of *i griega* (Greek i) and some minor adjustments which its co-ordinator Salvador Gutiérrez Ordóñez described as in keeping with common usage, reasonable, simple and understandable. The Mexican newspaper *El Universal* had this to say about the changed rules:

> Spelling is not just an imposition; it serves to maintain a minimum of coherence and sense to what is written and said. Can this be dictated from a conference room abroad? A country that is proudly independent would not accept this.[5]

Discuss this comment.

7 Writing and literacy in the digitalized world

Instant updates from your friends, industry experts, favourite celebrities, and what's happening around the world.[1]

DYKWUTB[2]

From the chosen through the initiated to everyone – admittedly rather compressed, but this in brief is the social history of writing from its beginnings to the present time. Writing has come a long way since its invention, but, notwithstanding the many changes it has undergone, it still is recognizably the same: the generation and recording of meaning in the visual mode. Yet the circumstances in which we make use of the written word are as different from those of Assyrian, Greek and Chinese antiquity as are the technologies employed then and now. The progression from clay tablets to touch screens is the path of civilization (Baron 2009), which has been welcomed and resisted, praised and cursed at every juncture along the way. The benefits of writing were highlighted by the Greek philosopher Diodoros (Siculus), who, in the first century BCE, underlined the great importance he assigned to it, stating that 'while it is true that nature is the cause of life, the cause of the *good* life is education based on the written word' (quoted from Harris 1989: 26). Millions of written pages later, Gottfried Leibniz (1646–1716), the greatest scholar of his time, who firmly believed in the perfectibility of humanity, was much more sceptical, expressing his fear that 'after uselessly exhausting curiosity without obtaining from our investigations any considerable gain for our happiness, people may be disgusted with the sciences, and that a fatal despair may cause them to fall back into barbarism. To which result that horrible mass of books which keeps on growing might contribute very much' (Leibniz 1680/1951: 29). On the other hand, there is, of course, no shortage of voices in praise of the written word, which has not only freed us from the limitations of human memory, but also expanded access to intellectual achievements. Its enthusiastic recommendation as an existential necessity by a writer such as Gustave Flaubert does not come as a surprise: 'But do not read, as children read, to amuse you, nor as the ambitious read, to enlighten yourself. No, read *to live*. Create in your mind an intellectual atmosphere made up of the emanations of all the great thinkers' (Dufour 2009; my translation). While this recommendation may convince many, especially those who grew up in the world of letters and make a living by contributing to it, the effects of writing are not equally beneficial for all. Cultural anthropologist Claude Lévi-Strauss who spent a lifetime studying the 'savage', that is, the non-literate mind, viewed literate civilization critically, arguing that 'my hypothesis, if correct, would oblige us to recognize the fact that the primary function of written communication is to facilitate slavery' (Lévi-Strauss 1973: 300). Careful study of the history of Western civilization and its effects on other cultures certainly lends support to such a pessimistic view. At the same time it must be admitted that a critical appraisal of the effects of writing would not be possible in the absence of writing and not just in the sense that you cannot criticize something that isn't there, but also, arguably, because writing enables us to see the world differently.

There is great complexity in the art and technology of writing. It can do good as well as harm. That was so in antiquity, and it is so today. Writing helped expand the capacity of the human mind and establish privilege, discrimination and oppression. It served the spread of both enlightenment and myths, science and religion, useful information and spam. Writing was instrumental in creating the great cultivated national languages, often at the expense of unwritten idioms that were pushed into oblivion. Yet, electronic writing technology for display and transmission of texts has greatly facilitated the writing of hitherto unwritten languages. Jack Goody (1977) was right when he described writing as a 'technology of the intellect', but his critics from the New Literacy Studies approach (Street 1995), who insist that literacy is not just an abstract set of reading and writing skills that are independent of any social, political and economic context, are also right. The development of writing and its effects on social evolution are dialectic, every technological improvement creating new possibilities of abuse and its rectification. And, we should hasten to add, what is abuse and what rectification often depends on the beholder.

The history of civilization has produced and continues to produce a multiplicity of literacies with different types of writing variously shaped by and embedded in different cultural contexts. However, in spite of these manifest differences, the power of the written word is such that no one can ignore it or evade it. It controls us as much as we control it. While individual relapse into illiteracy is a commonly observed feature of adult literacy campaigns, no community is known ever to have abandoned writing collectively after having been introduced to it. An indispensable instrument of social organization, execution of power and economic gain, it has shaped the world as it is today, and nothing suggests that another technological innovation will supersede it in the foreseeable future. Yet, as little as a few decades ago when the media revolution was just beginning to make itself felt, this was not so clear. For instance, writing in the early 1980s, Edward Corbett, a professor of English, asked: 'Will writing continue to play a significant role in the political, professional, cultural, and business affairs of our society during the last quarter of this century?' (1981: 47). He deemed it necessary to argue against the position 'that writing is an anachronism in our electronic age' (1981: 52). Such a stance seems cranky today but is, perhaps, understandable if we remember that at the time words such as 'mobile phone', 'SMS', 'blog', 'text message' and even 'e-mail' meant little or nothing to most people. In the meantime the undiminished multifarious importance of writing has become, if anything, more obvious. No doubts remain that, for better or worse – and remarkable progress in speech recognition and mind-reading research notwithstanding – the reliance of contemporary society on written language is greater than ever. Whither writing? This is the question around which the final chapter of this book revolves. As the New Literacy Studies would insist, no satisfactory answer can be expected unless we look beyond the technological implications of digitalized language. At issue is more than a new tool that allows us to do the same job as the old one, only better. We are dealing with a profound culture change with ramifications for language and society, economy and politics. This is too vast a canvas to be fully covered here. A discussion of some of the more momentous features of writing in the age of the Internet must suffice.

LANGUAGE AND COMPUTER-MEDIATED COMMUNICATION

First, language. Does language change under the influence of digitalization? It certainly does, as it did when TV talk shows first made their appearance; when radio broadcasting first made it possible to report in real time on happenings, such as sports events and political rallies, that the listeners could not see; when newspapers came into circulation; and when the printing press spurred literacy acquisition and language standardization. New media and writing tools always instigate linguistic innovations beyond the incessant pace of language change, innovations that are somehow specific to technological change. It is only to be expected that e-mail, e-forum posting, blogs, text messages, Tweets and

Figure 7.1 The writing on the wall

other electronic forms of writing give rise to new registers and stylistic variation. But the uses of language are many, and the forces of continuity that prevent a language from being transformed out of recognition are strong. What, then, are the changes that can be observed?

In the previous chapter I touched upon the question of whether spell-checkers will lead to the de-standardization of the most highly standardized languages, which happen to be the languages most widely used in computer-mediated communication (CMC). It takes time to determine whether such drastic change will be brought about by the increase of online text in the wake of word processing and Internet technology, and it is, therefore, premature to venture a definitive answer. But that language use is affected by these technologies is beyond doubt, and like any other observable change in linguistic usage the peculiarities of *internet speak* are dreaded by some as ruining our beloved tongue, whereas others CCL. There is a huge literature already investigating the linguistic consequences of CMC (e.g. Negroponto 1995; Baron 2008; Crystal 2001, 2008; Danet and Herring 2007; Eckkrammer and Eder 2000; Gottlieb

2011; Randall 2002), which is certain to keep growing as the differences between fashionable effects and longer-lasting consequences become more apparent. The bulk of this literature is about the written language, which is indicative of changes in linguistics as much as in language.

A long-standing debate in sociolinguistics is about the nature of standards, where they come from, and whether language standardization is possible without writing. Institutional norms of linguistic behaviour are established by higher-status groups and overtly promoted by language academies, schools and the media. While notions of right and wrong or deviant can be applied to vernacular speech, it is clear that language standardization was greatly aided by writing. Typically, the standard is encoded in primers, reference grammars and dictionaries, as discussed in Chapter 5. In contemporary society, community-wide recognition of the norms encoded in the standard across all social classes is usually acknowledged, the written language being expected to conform to the norm to a much higher degree than speech. The language community reacts with more tolerance to colloquial speech than to substandard writing. However, this is changing. Digital media have different implications for standardization from their predecessors. While printing with metal type favoured a rigid standard, digital desk-top printing allows for more flexibility, not to mention the infinite amount of written language production that is never printed but only appears on computer screens and displays. New forms of written communication evolve in ways that resemble those characteristic of vernacular speech.

Quasi-speech

Non-standard spellings are among the most conspicuous features of some kinds of CMC, especially instant messaging. While some conservative educators and commentators regard these deviances as exacerbating the problems of the general deterioration of the language and semi-literate secondary school learners, more detached analysts point out that unconventional spellings in this medium testify to inventiveness rather than incompetence (Tagliamonte and Denis 2008). Crystal points out the obvious, stating that 'Texters would not be able to use the mobile phone technology at all if they had not been taught to read and write, and this means that they all had a grounding in the standard English writing system' (Crystal 2008: 48). Deviant spellings are found more objectionable than nonchalant speech, precisely because sweat and tears were shed to learn the orthography and we, therefore, expect written texts to contain words in their standard spellings. This expectation is systematically breached in texting because, while written, this manner of communication is handled by its users as a form of

Table 7.1 *Texting jargon*

AFAIK	as far as I know
B4	before
CCL	couldn't care less
CU	see you
DNC	do not compute (don't understand)
F2F	face to face
G2TU	got to tell you
JTLYK	just to let you know
SPST	same place, same time
UR	you are
WRK	work
Y?	why

quasi – or conceptual orality. The fact that the telephone is the prototypical communication tool of oral-only exchange may have contributed to the hybrid character of instant messages (Simpson 2002) by way of incorporating features of conversational performance into writing once the handset was equipped with a visual display. Abercrombie, in an insightful paper about differences between speech and writing, remarked that 'writing is a device developed for recording prose, not conversation' (Abercrombie 1963: 14). Instant messaging was not even on the horizon when he wrote, and a chat was an (oral) conversation. In the meantime, features of conversational speech have seeped into writing, though less in terms of phonetic mimicry, such as eye dialect, than on the level of pragmatics and conversational dynamics. However, the affinity of text message production to speech has also been demonstrated on the word level. A quantitative analysis of textisms – that is, truncated words used in text messages – has revealed that frequent texters are more likely to create phonological textisms such as *cum, no, wot* for *come, know, what,* whereas less experienced texters use a higher proportion of orthographic textisms, such as *com, knw, wat,* retaining more orthographic features of the words in question (Kemp 2010).

Text messaging is the most widely used mobile data service worldwide. Since written texts conveyed by mobile phones were initially limited to a fixed number of characters per message, fanciful acronyms and hybrid words combining letters, ciphers and letter names proliferated.

Chopping up words and phrases to save key strokes and time is a strategy that has influenced this electronic register. With the advent of texting, similarly abbreviated and truncated forms emerged in many other languages; but the writing system has a modulating effect on the register features induced by the cell phone interface, providing an interesting manifestation of how writing system and technology interact in the creation of meaning. Gottlieb (2011) describes a number of characteristic practices of Japanese texting, such as the increased use of Chinese characters (kanji) instead of the usual mix of kanji and kana for the sake of saving space, and the playful use of alphabetic letters, Roman numerals and mathematical symbols, by which writers try to mimic or insinuate speech-like effects. It has furthermore been observed that social subgroups establish their own conventions of character usage that function much like youth and other jargons to strengthen network connections and in-group cohesion (Jaffe 2000). Gao Liwei reports similar findings characterizing Chinese Internet Language (CIL) as a written register used mostly by educated young urban Chinese which, he believes, because of its users' prestige, 'may spread to other age groups and beyond the CMC modality and consequently lead to changes in the Chinese language' (Gao 2008: 375). Gottlieb, while describing technology-related features of online communication in considerable detail, is more cautious as regards their effects on the language, arguing that these features are likely to be compartmentalized, 'called into service when using a cell phone or PC to send an email or blog post but not necessarily part of the user's writing habits in other areas' (2011: 148). As happened with other innovations of writing technology, CMC-induced changes are more likely to supplement rather than replace established features and modes of writing.

Among the more conspicuous changes noted by both Gottlieb and Gao are lexical innovations originating in SMS slang and cross-modality influences. The alphabetic keyboard has a noticeable effect on the two languages – Chinese and Japanese – noted, as evidenced, for instance, by acronyms that consist of the pronunciation of English letter names. This is a well-known strategy for brand names – such as *Bee Em Doubleyou*, *Bee Pee* and NHK, pronounced [en-aitʃ-kaj] from *nihon hōsō kyōkai* 'Japanese Broadcasting Corporation' – which has invaded the spoken language. For instance, [key wai] is a new word derived from the names of the letters K and Y in English and stands for the Japanese phrase *kūki yomenai* which means 'cannot read the air' and refers to people who cannot intuitively understand a situation. Similarly, *JS* is a Chinese acronym of *jianshang*, 'shrewd businessman'. These and many other neologisms bear testimony in speech to the input mode of CMC in Japanese and Chinese. While words of this sort are evidently a spin-off of digital writing technology, their influence on overall lexical innovation is modest. Influences of digitalization on other subsystems of the language, syntax and morphology in particular, are even harder to discern.

Stylistic diversification with several new registers and orthographic peculiarities is quite noticeable, but does not imply any obvious system-altering changes in the language.

What has changed, though, is the way we write. Writers who start the day by sharpening pencils and neatly aligning paper sheets on the desk are an endangered species, while most professional writers (and masses of non-professional ones) switch on their computer, which gives them access not just to spellcheckers and parsers, but to online dictionaries and an endless array of reference works, not to mention databases, daily news and their own archives. All this makes writing physically easier and lowers the barriers of class and education to clear writing. Thus, while word processing and Internet technology have a potential to undermine standards, they at the same time work to reinforce these same standards by democratizing access to written language.

A writing public

It is because of this dimension of broadening access to written language that word-processing software and Internet-based CMC have lasting effects on the handling of written language in society. Most consequential of all, especially for cellphone literacy practices, is that more people have taken to writing than ever before. Mass media, when they first appeared, were unidirectional: a few wrote, many read. But digital literacy means using devices for reading and writing, and also means that in many instances the temporal lag between writer and reader has been potentially eliminated. Writing something that others would read used to be the prerogative of those who controlled the languages and registers deemed suitable for writing.[3] With our own desktop publishing equipment at hand, and even more so when we visit a chat room or use a cellphone that, for the reasons explained above, gives licence to violate conventional spelling rules without any need to explain whether this is out of insufficient knowledge or choice, the threshold for expressing oneself in writing has been markedly lowered. Although teachers, publishers, editors and other gatekeepers are standing their ground, for now, the hugely increased writing community, a nascent writing public, is likely to have an effect on the future development of the written language, in the long run.

The function of written language as a social marker and the correlation of styles with social class will not disappear, but the further democratization of literacy will change the overall relationship between social hierarchy and language use. Spell-check software has changed the way we write. For handwriting and typing the writer had to know the correct spelling of a word before writing it down, while for writing in the CMC mode selecting the correct alternative from a set of options is sufficient. At the same time the universal availability of this software in the most advanced countries has made spelling mistakes in serious texts such as term papers, résumés, formal letters, etc., even less excusable than they formerly were.

Technological innovations often find unanticipated applications. When mobile phones became widely available in the Philippines, a 90 per cent Christian country, many young people found it convenient to confess their sins by text messages or e-mail. However, this attempt to replace an oral communication event by writing was stopped in its tracks. Bishops, citing the issue of confidentiality, would not give absolution by electronic messaging.

Or, to take another example, who would have predicted the birth of the mobile-phone novel at the beginning of the century? Whether earlier attempts were made and failed is not known, but when, in 2003, Yoshi published *Deep Love*,[4] a novel composed on a mobile phone and intended to be read on one, it became a hit immediately with millions of Japanese readers. That Japan was the original birthplace of this genre was hardly coincidental. Information density of kanji (Chinese characters) and kana (syllabic signs) is higher than for alphabetic writing, and at the time penetration of mobile phones with Internet access was higher there than in any other country. The fact that Japan is a commuter society where people spend plenty of time on trains playing with their mobile phones may also have contributed to the great popularity of mobile-phone novels, which, however, also spread to other parts of East Asia. Though they were shunned by literary critics as worse than pulp fiction, these novels epitomized the trend of bringing to writing sections of the public that before CMC would never have dreamt of writing books.

From word of mouth to word of mouse

That technology enables people to write whatever they fancy not only allows them to ignore redundant letters, majuscules, apostrophes and other niceties of orthography, but also makes it possible to write any variety or language, no matter whether it has an established written norm or has ever been reduced to writing at all. The web is patient, and it has become multilingual (Danet and Herring 2007). If we think about the consequences of digitalization for language, it is important to include this unintended and unexpected potential of online communication, which has been put to use by many linguistic minorities.

Counting languages and dialects is an old problem that embarrasses linguists and cannot be resolved without reference to non-linguistic criteria, as discussed in Chapter 3. The digitalization of texts and their accessibility in cyberspace has made it possible to count all sorts of things, but not languages. There are websites such as *Internet World Stats* that track the frequency of occurrence of a number of languages in the Internet,[5] and the Unicode Consortium prides itself on 'enabl[ing] people around the world to use computers in any language' (www.unicode.org/). Implicit in this assertion is the qualification 'any language recognized as such', a point to which I will return presently, but, first, notice that the technology also supports written communication in unconventional varieties that do not meet the standards for recognition as a language. Examples include using a Romanized script for writing culturally displaced languages, such as Arabic, Farsi, Greek, Punjabi and Urdu in immigrant communities (e.g. Themistocleous 2010; Rosowsky 2010; Anand n.d.). In many immigrant settings the home language is used primarily orally, the younger generation not being instructed in its usual script and orthography. The Roman script of the school language, English, French, Dutch, for example, is in such cases used 'as a pedagogical "shortcut"' (Rosowsky 2010: 163) or because the speakers have never learnt the native script and orthography, but still want to use their in-group language in CMC.

A community whose life has been profoundly affected by CMC generally and text messaging in particular are the deaf. The cellphone has liberated them from the face-to-face situations required for signing and from relying on hearing people for communication. Thus even in their own homes deaf people can now communicate from one room to another, enabling them to be more independent and flexible. CMC technology opens up new possibilities for the deaf, but also brings a question to the fore that was not unknown, but has been largely ignored for a long time: the question, that is, of which language to write. The most common practice is using the dominant spoken language (DSL) for writing, that is, English, French, Korean, etc. However, this solution amounts to a rather extreme form of diglossia: signing one language and writing another. The alternative is SignWriting, that is, using writing systems to encode signed language (Figure 7.2). Various such systems have been developed (Hopkins 2008; Arnold and Nakatsui 2010), but so far signed language writing has not made much headway, because deaf communities have not shown much interest, because not many documents are available, and because launching any new notation is an uphill battle. The Internet has made it much easier to establish discussion groups investigating and experimenting with SignWriting.

The same holds for many other communities of lesser-used languages that, while finding themselves increasingly at the margin of global communication flows, at the same time are taking advantage of the ultimate

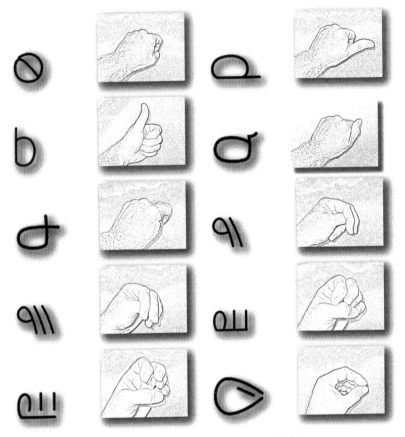

Figure 7.2 Sample of American Sign Language Writing

tool of globalization, the Internet, for their own purposes, documenting their languages and making available written materials that would
otherwise be forgotten on the shelves of a provincial library. For writing pidgins and other substandard varieties, too, the Internet gives a
new lease of life (Taavitsainen, Melchers and Pahta 2000), for Internet
users are not bound by any standard and are free to use the technology to create and express attitudes and social and cultural identities
shifting between standard and non-standard varieties much more flex-
ibly than used to be possible in writing for other than entirely private
purposes.

An expanded writing community and the technological capacity to
write any language do not mean that all standards have been abolished,

leaving the Internet as an anarchic free-for-all. In connection with the problem of language recognition mentioned above (p. 135), the International Standard Organisation has defined criteria for requesting new language codes (ISO 639) from which it can be deduced what counts as a language in the eyes of the ISO. The main points are here quoted in full:

- *Number of documents.* The request for a new language code shall include evidence that one agency holds 50 different documents in the language or that five agencies hold a total of 50 different documents among them in the language. Documents include all forms of material and are not limited to text.
- *Collective codes.* If the criteria above are not met the language may be assigned a new or existing collective language code. The words *languages* or *other* as part of a language name indicates that a language code is a collective one.
- *Scripts.* A single language code is normally provided for a language even though the language is written in more than one script. ISO DIS 15924 *Codes for the representation of names of scripts* is under development by ISO/TC46/SC2.
- *Dialects.* A dialect of a language is usually represented by the same language code as that used for the language. If the language is assigned to a collective language code, the dialect is assigned to the same collective language code. The difference between dialects and languages will be decided on a case-by-case basis.
- *Orthography.* A language using more than one orthography is not given multiple language codes. (www.loc.gov/standards/iso639–2/ iso639jac_n3r.html)

The ISO criteria are immaterial for private and semi-private communication of small groups pursuing their own designs or determined to promote a language not otherwise used in writing. For minorities seeking official recognition, however, these criteria may be important, as status may imply subsidies, government services and immaterial support. ISO 639 does not solve the sociolinguistic problems of language status determination, but it is manifest proof that these problems have been carried over from the age of printed text into the age of texting and other forms of CMC where they are being redefined. In brief, the Internet has changed the day-to-day reality in which writing is embedded.

THE NEW ECONOMICS OF WRITING

Second, the economy. From an economic point of view, the crucial issue of writing in the age of the Internet is consumption of globalized digital content. In the knowledge economy, digital content is an increasingly important and valuable commodity, not limited to written language but, when it comes to technical, scientific and practical information, clearly dominated by it. And the capacity to produce well-designed text is a marketable component of human capital that feeds more people than ever in the history of humanity. Since the 1950s, consumer capitalism, first in the USA and Europe and subsequently spreading around the globe, has brought about far-reaching cultural transformations. That ad writing has been elevated to the level of graduate courses is among the most significant and iconic. In the Western economies of overproduction, advertising has become a 'creative industry' and a 'social technology' (Hartley 2009) that not only drives innovation and change, but also has invaded the domain of social exchange, having become a pervasive element of the public sphere (Kasapi 2009). And it is a huge and growing part of the knowledge-based economy (OECD 1996)[6] measured in billions of dollars. In 2011, total advertising expenditure in the USA, the biggest spender, amounted to US$ 316 billion, the same order of magnitude as the total government expenditure of Russia (US$ 341 billion). Not all of it is for text, but print media and Internet ads taken together account for about 50 per cent. To quote another figure, the volume of the merger of Time-Warner with Internet provider AOL in 2001 was estimated at US$ 183 billion; written language is a consumer staple of both companies.

Thus, writing is big business. This is obvious if we look just at the field of commercial advertising, and there are, of course, many other manifestations, such as newspapers, magazines, manuals, technical reports, catalogues, textbooks, children's books, religious books, dictionaries, cookbooks, etc. The amount of written material being produced and traded in the global market place continues to grow, stimulating the development of new technologies for storing, distributing and managing texts (Heller 2003). Each successive generation of writing technology expands the amount of written material, and as the quote from Leibniz near the beginning of this chapter suggests, this increase has often been perceived as a threat to quality. Accordingly, finding the information we need without being too much distracted by marginal or unrelated materials has become more urgent as well as more difficult.

In a report in 1996, the OECD mentioned the following elements of an emerging, universally accessible library: 'a vast array of public and private information sources, including digitised reference volumes, books, scientific journals, libraries of working papers, images, video clips, sound and voicerecordings, graphical displays as well as electronic mail...connected through various communications networks' (OECD

1996: 13). This cyberspace library, universally accessible in the most advanced countries and increasingly in less-developed countries as well, has become a reality and continues to grow. The volume of written material is daunting. Digitalization does not improve our ability to read, although it facilitates access to the books we want to read, saving us a trip to the library or bypassing time-consuming interlibrary loans, for example. However, assume you have another eighty years to live and, having successfully completed a speed-reading course, you decide to devote the rest of your life to reading a book a day. You could only read about as many books as are published every year in Viet Nam, some 25,000. UNESCO considers the number of new titles published per country per year as an important index of standard of living and education and therefore monitors and publishes comparative statistics. Viet Nam, a country that for decades has boasted high literacy rates, ranks 18th on a list of 110 countries in terms of book production. Statistics are incomplete, outdated for some countries and overall not very reliable, one of the lesser problems being that there is no easy answer to the question of what should count as a book.[7] However, if figures are added up we arrive at more than a million new books published annually, give or take a few hundred thousand – the UK, China and Germany being the market leaders. Book publishing is on the retreat, while the market for e-books is growing. Many publishers now release all of their new publications in digital as well as print format, as reading behaviour is changing. Given this overwhelming mass of publications and the vastly increased accessibility of scientific, educational and cultural materials, ancillary tools for screening, indexing, summarizing, cross-referencing and translating texts become ever more important, sustaining subsidiary industries.

Editing and desktop publishing, creating and updating databases, verifying sources and detecting plagiarism, bibliometric research, tapping data flows in the Internet to analyse trends for commercial, political and scholarly ends, filtering and systematizing contents from every conceivable point of view – these are just some of the software applications built on sophisticated methods of written language analysis. Tweets, blogs and Facebook pages supply an inexhaustible amount of information for analysis, social media having drawn the habits, feelings and preferences of hundreds of millions of people into the public domain.

It is a hazard of writing about technological innovation that the speed of change easily outstrips that of the analysis. Benign readers will perhaps forgive me for reminding them that this is a book, not a blog, which is why I refrain from citing any statistics about the capacity to store, retrieve, compute and communicate information[8] or about the growing market share of e-books, the increasing volume of e-mail traffic and electronic data interchange, texting and other forms of computer-mediated communication, and the skyrocketing distribution of malware. Comments about the latest communication gadgets are equally risky. Using a cellphone not equipped with a news alarm and a personal assistant with speech synthesizer that, spontaneously, tells me whether or not I should take an umbrella with me when I go to the office in the morning, I look medieval to my daughter. At the same time, in doing my daily work I use writing technologies, both software and hardware, that were beyond imagination when I went to college. Technological change has never been so fast-paced. In the wake of the transition from typing to word-processing, and again when the Internet became accessible to wider circles, first on stationary computers and then on mobile devices, the worldwide flow of information in business and culture has steadily grown and accelerated, speeding up the cycles of technological innovation in turn. In addition to printing and publishing, processing written language has become an economically significant business with many ramifications in culture, society and politics. For IT engineers it is of secondary importance whether the information being stored and computed is textual, vocal, pictorial or numerical, as they are concerned with electrons flowing through cyberspace rather than meaning. From the point of view of this book, however, it is important to emphasize that nothing rivals the written word as a vehicle of generating, storing and communicating meaning, and that the new technologies have reinforced rather than diminished its preeminent position. Digitalization has vastly expanded its reach, creating new fields of economic activity. There is nothing at the horizon that rivals its cultural significance, and economically the importance of written language has also grown steadily as the transformation from the industrial to a knowledge-based economy proceeds, for the accumulation, effective communication, dissemination and processing of information relies to a large extent on written text – on a printed page, computer screen, digital reader or mobile-phone display. Other forms of knowledge, such as tacit know-how of organizational structures and procedures and operating complex machinery, are no less important, but are not so easily turned into market commodities or economic resources. All told, in the knowledge stock of society, the economic importance of written language has steadily increased ever since universal literacy has been recognized as an objective of social development. The digital revolution has not changed that.

A TRANSFORMED PUBLIC SPHERE

Third, politics. Profound changes were brought about by the digital revolution also in the political sphere, involving, among other things, the functions of writing and written language in society. As we have seen in Chapter 2, the public sphere of modernity was a 'read-only' public sphere. CMC and mass access to the Internet have made the public sphere more interactive, transforming it into a reading and writing public. Search engines, social-network websites, collective information sites, dating sites, eBusiness websites, online chat rooms, forums, blogs, web reviews, mailing lists, to mention just the most common arenas of online behaviour, all require active participation. In one way or another users engage in these activities by providing a written input. E-democracy, too, is beginning to take shape, as local forums promote civic engagement online, government agencies deliver ever more services to citizens online, and online voting is moving beyond the experimental stage in many countries.

Further, new media have in various ways influenced civil society, as distinct from government and private business (Fischer 2006). The Internet has created a virtual space where activist groups and NGOs can constitute themselves, share information and get organized. It has been argued, for instance, that after the devastating earthquake and tsunami of 11 March 2011 in Eastern Japan vital information was distributed through social-network sites, compensating for normal infrastructure channels that had been destroyed in wide areas. While gathering and distributing information about missing people, shelters, etc., was universally welcomed, the role of the new media was not quite so unproblematic, as the natural catastrophe was followed by the nuclear power plant incident that forced tens of thousands of people to evacuate. Many groups and individuals began publishing radiation measurements, not all of them authorized or qualified to do so. Two unwelcome consequences ensued: trust in government sources was undermined, and people suffered from an overflow of information. Both of these problems are symptomatic of the sociopolitical effects of instant communication rather than being specific to the natural disaster in Japan. Common access to information is likely to undermine trust in official and otherwise certified sources, whereas the greatly increased variety and quantity of available data pose new challenges to the public in selecting from and evaluating them.

Another example of how non-state actors made use of new communication technologies with far-reaching consequences for social and

Figure 7.3 Then: Speaker's Corner in London, 1933, addressing those within earshot

political happenings was the so-called Arab Spring of 2011 (Al Lawati 2011). Initially it was likened to the student demonstrations that rocked Beijing in 1989, but there was a big difference: social network media were not yet available then. 'The 1989 movement ... lacked any organized media "voice of the students". [It] was strong on mobilization and found deep popular sympathy, but it fell behind on both theory and communication' (Calhoun 1989: 25). In marked contrast to the Tiananmen protest, the wave of rebellions and demonstrations in the Arab world that started in late December 2010 in Tunisia relied heavily on Internet communications and social-network tools, which are said to have contributed to these uprisings on two levels. First, Internet-savvy youths used social-network sites to spread information and organize rallies, repeatedly circumventing government attempts to shut down websites and servers. Especially in the uprising which began on 25 January 2011 in Egypt, digital platforms had a political impact, being instrumental in mobilizing demonstrators and co-ordinating their activities. It is because of this potential that satellites, computers and video cameras were hailed as 'technologies of freedom' (Sola Pool 1984) decades ago. Controlling the press and shutting down broadcasting

Figure 7.4 Now: WikiLeaks, 2010, addressing the world

stations is easier than policing the Internet, but as with all new technologies, new uses and abuses become possible. There are hackers working for and against the regime, be it in Syria or the United States.

The second way in which Internet communication had an impact on the Arab Spring was the release by WikiLeaks of a number of US diplomatic cables that made Arab leaders appear as Washington's lackeys. Taken up in other media, these revelations fuelled resentment against Arab governments in the masses beyond the student population. This was an interesting moment in the history of communications, as a new technology was applied in a way that compromised those who had devised it and thought that they could fully control it. Not much praise was heard in this connection about a technology of freedom – not anyway on the part of those who are bent on maintaining and expanding their domination of Internet content, the cultural industry and government of the United States. The hostility WikiLeaks' activities have met from the American establishment is reminiscent of the Pope's condemnation of the printing press in the sixteenth century, which made Christian scriptures accessible to the masses and thus posed a challenge to the church's exclusive licence of interpretation and the control of public morality. The same technology holds the potential to repress and to liberate. The interesting point here is not the double standard and hypocrisy, but rather the wishful thinking of those who believe that they can harness the technology for their own ends, 'setting the terms and conditions of an emerging world information order' (Howley 2005: 27). Calling the Internet a technology of freedom is, therefore, a doubtful proposition. What can be said is that it is the ultimate plebeian technology, having opened the floodgates not just for leaks but for everything, good and bad, no matter by what standards, to be given the chance to find a reader.

Julian Assange, founder and head of WikiLeaks, is only the messenger who happens to have understood the zeitgeist and the nature of the technology that now determines the flow of information around the globe. The soapbox at Speaker's Corner (Figure 7.3) is no longer an important platform of free *speech*; the Internet is. And free speech is not the only point at issue: transparency and the denial of information monopolies are just as important – and as important as was the denial of the interpretation monopoly of the church fostered by the printing press and the spread of literacy at the threshold of modernity. WikiLeaks, which was initiated in 2006 and which shot to worldwide prominence in 2010 (Figure 7.4), embodies what it means to be living in an information society (Garnham 2000). It has become both easier and faster to distribute knowledge committed to writing as well as more difficult to hide matters of public interest from the public. The Internet provides the technical framework to which societies are only beginning to adjust. WikiLeaks' merit is that it has dragged hackers and whistle-blowers from shady corners on the fringe of legality onto a respectable stage of championing democracy. Many things will have to be rethought as a result, including copyright, authorship, protection of sources, censorship and privacy, to mention but the most obvious.

In a situation where anything can be published not just locally but worldwide at any time and in real time, new answers are being sought to the questions of where full transparency is necessary and where it is preferable and viable to restrict access to information or its distribution. Established institutions, no matter where, tend to favour limitations, on one pretext or another – protecting the lives of one's secret agents, shielding the innocent from immoral material, preventing blasphemy, non-interference in government operations, fighting illegal content, etc. There are indications that governments are very uncertain as to how to handle the flow of information through the Internet, among them the uproar about WikiLeaks' threat to US government secrecy and the fact that, since the beginning of the century, the number of governments censoring the Internet has increased substantially.[9] An undeclared arms race is taking place between governments developing software to repress and censor, and activists working to thwart them.[10] The story of WikiLeaks epitomizes these developments, but it should not be overrated. Even if its adversaries succeed in silencing Julian Assange and his friends, it will be well-nigh impossible to plug the leak that he opened. WikiLeaks has inspired any number of copycat leak sites, such as CorporateLeaks, GlobalLeaks, OpenLeaks, CrowdLeaks, UniLeaks, Israel-Leaks, SaudiLeaks, EnviroLeaks, HackerLeaks, among others, all of which are dedicated to publishing content that someone does not want to be published. This profoundly affects the way politics is done, on the part of both governments and governed.

The effects of CMC on politics cannot be charted here in detail. For our purposes, it is important to emphasize the new role of literacy in politics. The Arab Spring was the most *literate* political movement ever in that part of the world and would not have been possible until recently. For instance, in Tunisia where the movement began, the promotion of mass education was a phenomenon of the 1990s (Walters 2003: 85–7). In the age of the Internet it has become more difficult for autocratic regimes to ignore public opinion, and it is not just in countries with autocratic regimes that the political game changes. In market democracies, too, communication technology developments, most notably the personal computer and the mobile phone in conjunction with social-network tools, have fundamentally altered the manner in which writing is prac-tised in society. Although the revealing power of photographs and video clips of power abuse cannot be denied, the bulk of communication on social-network sites and leak sites feared by the powers that be is written communication.

In the 'read-only' public sphere, writing was a means of persuasion, be it for political propaganda campaigns or commercial advertising cam-paigns, controlled largely by governments or commercial, profit-seeking media systems. Although the multiplicity of written material allowed attentive readers to protect themselves against being reduced to help-less victims of ideological conditioning, the means to influence public opinion were heavily tilted in favour of those who controlled the chan-nels of communication. The interactive potential of Internet-mediated communication does not change property and power relations, but it holds the potential to change the way that public opinion is formed and, most importantly, translated into action. Technology has increased rather than reduced the importance of writing for political information and participation. Political protests from the Arab Spring to the Occupy (Wall Street) movement have demonstrated that and shown that in combination with cellphones and personal computers, writing changes not just how people do business and connect with friends, but also the way they understand their position in society. The repercussions of the newly formed public sphere in the age of the Internet on the political process are only beginning to emerge.

CONCLUSIONS

In the age of the Internet and computer-mediated communication, writing and literacy acquire new forms and functions with many implications for language and culture as well as the economy and politics. Although most readers of this book hardly remember a world without the Internet, the media revolution is still quite new, the World Wide Web having been launched only in 1990. Thus, the handling of writing and written language under CMC conditions is still in the innovation and experimentation phase, exhibiting some unresolved contradictions. Quantity affects quality along several dimensions. One is that, as the number of Internet users worldwide, in 2011, has passed the 2 billion mark, more people and a greater share of the overall population in many countries have taken to handling written symbols actively rather than being passive recipients only. Hence, more people than ever contribute to shaping written language(s). At the same time, also in 2011, the world saw the birth of its seven billionth inhabitant. If we disregard children up to the age of fourteen as Internet users, which in advanced countries is not at all warranted, the world population is still three times that of Internet users, serving as a reminder that the digital divide persists and the gap in terms of written language skills and opportunities between the most and the least developed countries is wider than ever. This is a contradictory development that follows the logic of advancing the commercialization of written language production discussed above.

Another dimension of digital literacy where quantity affects quality has to do with time. Until recently, writing meant communication with a time lag, and for many genres this still holds. A correlative of the time lag vs co-presence contrast used to be that writing was meant to last, whereas speech was ephemeral. On a continuum between spontaneous and planned communication practices, unmonitored casual speech was at one end, and thought-out, repeatedly edited text at the other, with various mixed forms in-between. The synchronicity of certain forms of CMC changes the make-up of this continuum. As the written word migrates from paper to touch screen, it takes on an immediacy not previously associated with it, bringing a quasi-orality into existence. While the primary meaning of 'chat' has shifted from voiced talk to written online exchange and huge amounts of unedited casual language are committed to writing, the communicative differences between speech and writing are also affected. Although informal writing was hardly unknown previously, more individuals produce more writing than ever without any pretensions that it will last. *Verba volant, scripta manent* (spoken words fly away, written words stay), a Latin dictum that has held good since antiquity, is no longer valid. Yet there is another contradiction to note: while much electronic writing is not meant to be printed out or to be preserved in any other form, every word entrusted to the Internet leaves ineradicable traces behind. The information society has yet to come to grips with this contradiction.

Velocity and half-life are yet other temporal aspects of digital literacy. Whereas, as little as a few decades ago, it could take weeks to procure a book or document for inspection, no scientist or writer seriously involved in the business of producing texts can afford to wait more than days or hours any more. Books printed on paper continue to be written, but in other genres such as handwritten letters and CVs, the requirements of speed have all but driven out traditional manifestations of literacy. Expectations of swift response, 'swift' meaning within hours, puts correspondents and other writers under much pressure, some believe at the expense of thinking things through at leisure. The resources we have at our disposal without getting up from our desk have greatly changed the way we write, certainly increasing our productivity, but also, perhaps, reducing the half-life of books and research papers. These are difficult to measure, but everyone feels that the speed of digital data transmission affects how we handle written language: producing, processing and storing it.

Another contradiction of writing in the digital age is that easier access to more written material makes it more difficult to process. The increased speed of digital communication coincides with the increased amount of text the inhabitants of the society of letters are expected to process. At the upper end of literacy, this has implications for how we do science and what we can do. For researchers in advanced countries, staying abreast of current research in their field is no longer a problem of obtaining the relevant literature; filtering the information flood has become a much greater challenge. The overabundance of knowledge encoded in writing makes the demand for tools that enable us to use it in meaningful ways ever more urgent. At the same time, digitalization has opened new possibilities for empirical, corpus-based quantitative research in all scientific disciplines working with written materials.[11] Speed of transmission, amount of written material and storage space interact to define a new information environment to which *Homo*

ENCYCLOPÉDIE,

O U

DICTIONNAIRE RAISONNÉ

DES SCIENCES,

DES ARTS ET DES MÉTIERS,

PAR UNE SOCIÉTÉ DE GENS DE LETTRES.

Mis en ordre & publié par M. *DIDEROT,* de l'Académie Royale des Sciences & des Belles-Lettres de Prusse ; & quant à la PARTIE MATHÉMATIQUE, par M. *D'ALEMBERT,* de l'Académie Royale des Sciences de Paris, de celle de Prusse, & de la Société Royale de Londres.

Tantùm series juncturaque pollet,
Tantùm de medio sumptis accedit honoris ! HORAT.

TOME PREMIER.

A PARIS,

Chez
BRIASSON, *rue Saint Jacques, à la Science.*
DAVID l'aîné, *rue Saint Jacques, à la Plume d'or.*
LE BRETON, Imprimeur ordinaire du Roy, *rue de la Harpe.*
DURAND, *rue Saint Jacques, à Saint Landry, & au Griffon.*

M. DCC. LI.

AVEC APPROBATION ET PRIVILEGE DU ROY.

Figure 7.5 Then: Denis Diderot's *Encyclopédie*, 1750

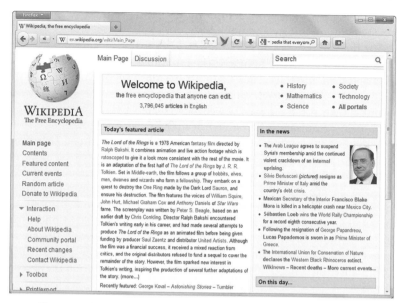

Figure 7.6 Now: an encyclopedia that anyone can edit

sapiens, whose intellectual capacities haven't changed much since possessing a single book was the privilege of a few, must adjust.

At the lower end of literacy, digital technology has the potential of working as a great equalizer. Mass participation in social networks and forums makes it easier to find information on a topic, although sorting out the useful from the irrelevant presupposes a level of sophistication. The Internet does not distinguish between official, quality-controlled and individual texts. Everyone has the ability to contribute as well as to consume, an ability that, within the framework of social-network communication, is being transformed into an obligation. Peer pressure among friends is a reality also in the world of virtual Friends. Many young people feel that their social recognition depends strongly on their ability and willingness to tell their Friends something, however banal, on their Facebook site. Doing so, they contribute to another unresolved contradiction of Internet literacy in our day. Facebook communication is a private affair among friends, but it is no secret that what people have posted on their 'Wall' can be held against them, for instance, by potential employers. What is more, many users, politicians in particular, maintain Facebook accounts with thousands of Friends. The messages they post for their Friends to read are hardly private communication in the traditional sense of the word. However, it is precisely this sense that is changing. Social-network communication forces a redefinition of the divide between private and public.

For the young – say, today's high school entrants – communication in a semi-public private sphere is the point of departure which defines their position in society and the most obvious way of participating in community life. It is their online behaviour that must be studied if we want to understand the ways of writing in society today. To them, rather than being a nuisance, it is a fact of life that writing takes place in a commercial environment where ads pop up all around them. They also consider it a matter of fact that communication in the written mode is not a one-way street and that writing can be just as informal and short-lived as speech. They do not hesitate to submit their compositions, be it their life stories, a record of their everyday chores, comments on current events, or intellectual contributions to the blogosphere, to an anonymous or only partly acquainted readership, ready to accept suggestions for improvement. Even that they may be able and entitled to enhance the collective knowledge of the species is a notion they grow up with.

These are, indeed, very different perspectives for the uses of writing from those that have obtained since the beginning of mass literacy in the Enlightenment movement. No work better epitomized the drive to use writing for the edification of all people than Denis Diderot's *Encyclopédie* (Figure 7.5), which challenged the authorities of the absolutist state and therefore set the European bourgeoisie atwitter with excitement in the eighteenth century. It was intended to assemble all human knowledge and to allow everyone who might seek it any knowledge of the world. Underlying the project was the idea that specialists would provide the knowledge and offer it, in writing, to the reading public. Which leads us to a final contradiction. Since Diderot, knowledge has accumulated steadily. As a result things have become very complex and we depend increasingly on specialist knowledge not just in science, but in regard to many matters that affect our everyday lives. Yet, and this is the apparent contradiction, the most widely used reference work relies on collective intelligence. The obvious 21st-century answer to Diderot's *Encyclopédie* is, of course, Wikipedia, 'the free encyclopedia that anyone can edit' (Figure 7.6).

QUESTIONS FOR DISCUSSION

1 What are the characteristic stylistic differences between personal e-mail and online chatting?

2 What are the pros and cons of dissociating languages and their traditional writing systems in CMC?

3 The HTML lang attribute can be used to declare the language of a Web page or a portion of a Web page. This is meant to assist search engines and browsers. ISO 639-1 lists 165 language attributes and their codes (www.w3schools.com/tags/ref_language_codes.asp). Check the list and think about languages to add and why they should be added.

4 *Verba volant, scripta manent* was a cliché in European antiquity. How has its meaning since changed?

Notes

1 The tyranny of writing and the dominance of vernacular speech

1 Article 26 of the Universal Declaration of Human Rights stipulates that 'Everyone has the right to education. Education shall be free, at least in the elementary and fundamental stages' (www.un.org/en/documents/udhr/index.shtml#a26). This is the basis of framing the discourse on literacy within a human rights approach, for literacy is at the heart of basic education for all, and essential for ensuring sustainable development and eradicating poverty.

2 As early as the 1960s the head of the Phonetics Department of Edinburgh University, David Abercrombie, pointed out that the proclaimed priority of speech was not really implemented in linguistic research: 'We are constantly told that the main business of linguistics . . . is the investigation of spoken language; this is a point which has been especially strongly insisted on during the last 75 or so years. But what in fact linguistics has concerned itself with, up to now, has almost exclusively been – spoken prose. This is true of phonetics as well as all the rest of linguistics' (Abercrombie 1963: 12).

3 For an overview of Bernstein's theory of language codes and a critical assessment, see Sadovnik (1995).

4 www.physicalgeography.net/fundamentals/8e.html.

5 Upward- and downward-pointing arrows indicate rising and falling intonation, respectively, while numbers in brackets show lengths of pauses in seconds.

2 The past in the present and the seeds of the public sphere

1 An upright stone with an inscribed surface erected as a monument.

2 A larger-than-life copy of the Rosetta Stone by Joseph Kosuth adorns the floor of the museum dedicated to Jean-François Champollion in his birthplace, Figeac, France.

3 Koller is quoting Calhoun (2002).

4 See Backhaus (2007) for a thorough up-to-date review of linguistic landscape research; also Gorter (2006).

3 Written and unwritten language

1 *Chambers 21st Century Dictionary*, www.chambersharrap.co.uk/chambers/features/chref/chref.py/main?title=21st&query=patois.

4 Literacy and inequality

1 www.oecd.org/document/2/0,3343,en_2649_39263294_2670850_1_1_1_1,00.html.

2 Except on illiterate Whites whose fathers or grandfathers had exercised the right to vote. The so-called 'Grandfather Clause' was used in Southern states of the USA to provide exemption from literacy tests for illiterate Whites.

5 The society of letters

1 This reflects common usage in English of the word *Pharisee*, rather than the historical reality concerning differences between Pharisaic and other currents of Judaism.
In Christian scriptures the Pharisees are portrayed in their arguments with Jesus
as people who place the letter above the spirit of the law.

2 Lewis Carroll, *Through the Looking-Glass*. London: Macmillan, 1871, p. 205.

3 It is hardly fortuitous that the authors of the two most widely used dictionaries of legal usage, David Mellikoff (1992) and Bryan Garner (1995), both ardent
proponents of plain language, are (were) lawyers.

4 See, for instance, PLAIN, the Plain Language Association International, www.
plainlanguagenetwork.org/Organizations/index.html.

5 Proverbially, that is in the Book of Revelation 1,8, KJV.

6 Hephzibah Israel, quoted in Omoniyi (2010: 7), investigated Bible translation in
South India and found that a split in the community was invariably expressed in
terms of different translations of the Bible.

7 Lolcat, from Lol = 'laughing out loud' plus 'cat', is a made-up written variety
derived from English supposedly used by funny speaking cats. A written form of
communication much like Pig Latin, it has in recent years gained a wide following
in the Internet. Online English to Lol Cat translators can be found, as well as
various texts. One of the most ambitious projects is a full Bible translation into Lol
Cat: www.lolcatbible.com/index.php?title=John_1.

8 Spelling Your Way to S-u-c-c-e-s-s, *Island Family*. www.islandfamilymagazine.com/
aio-spelling-bee/island-family-march-2011/spelling-your-way-to-s-u-c-c-e-s-s.

9 The tendency to stick to a traditional practice even though better alternatives are
available.

6 Writing reform

1 'The utility that a subscriber derives from a communications service increases as
others join the system. This is a classic case of external economies in consumption
and has fundamental importance for the economic analysis of the communications
industry' (Rohlfs 1974: 16).

2 See www.spellingsociety.org/aboutsss/leaflets/intro.php.

3 But see also Morris (2010), who proposes that the underlying forces not just of the
history of writing, but of human history *tout court*, are sloth, greed and fear.

4 www.merrycoz.org/books/spelling/SPELLING.HTM.

5 *The Language Magazine*, December 2010, 14. (www.languagemagazine.com).

7 Writing and literacy in the digitalized world

1 Twitter's slogan.

2 Do you know what you are talking about?

3 This is not to deny the existence or importance of vernacular literacy, which,
however, in pre-modern Europe as well as in post-colonial situations, was never
integrated into the mainstream of literacy practices (see, e.g., Tabouret-Keller
et al. 1997).

4 For those who want to browse, here is a reference: http://view.books.yahoo.co.jp/
dor/drm/dor_main.php?key1=dexihhpu02-0002&sp=-1&ad=1&re=0&xmlurl=
http%3A%2F%2Fmaster.stream.books.yahoo.co.jp%3A8001%2F&shd=b7721dea
011dd9e01e6a4b5f430809b6e4cad30a.

5 At the time of writing, in autumn 2011, Chinese was hot on the heels of
English as the most widely used language in the Internet, followed by Spanish, Japanese, Portuguese, German, Arabic, French, Russian and Korean (www.
internetworldstats.com/stats7.htm).

6 A distinction is commonly made between 'knowledge industry', which produces knowledge, and 'knowledge-based industry', which uses knowledge as a resource. For present purposes the distinction is of lesser importance, for knowledge as both resource and commodity is for the most part made available in the form of written language.

7 Software engineer Leonid Taycher, who is involved in Google's Books of the World project, explains some of the finer points of dealing with publishing statistics: http://booksearch.blogspot.com/2010/08/books-of-world-stand-up-and-be-counted.html.

8 Hilbert and López (2011) offer a number of instructive statistics about the development of digital technologies since the 1990s.

9 When it comes to censoring the Internet, it is usually countries such as China and Iran that feature in Western media. That Germany, France, India, Poland and Spain are high on the ranking list of countries that request the removal of content from Google services and the handing over of user data is rarely reported. See www.google.com/transparencyreport/governmentrequests/.

10 When WikiLeaks uses the Internet to expose American machinations, it is evil; when US Secretary of State Clinton tells the social networking site Twitter to postpone online maintenance, as she did in 2009, so that the site would be available for Iranian anti-government protesters, it is for the best of humanity. When activists turn not against the Iranian or Egyptian governments but against the Pentagon and the US Department of State, they are accused of high treason.

11 See, for example, the 'culturomics' project investigating cultural trends quantitatively on the basis of a corpus of 5,195,769 digitized books containing about 4 per cent of all books ever published (Michel *et al.* 2010).

Bibliography

All internet sources cited in this book were verified in July 2012.

Abercrombie, David. 1963. Conversation and Spoken Prose. *ELT Journal* 18 (1), 10–16.

AIROÉ. 2000. *Le petit livre de l'orthographe actuelle, d'après le rapport du Conseil Supérieur de la Langue Française, documents administratifs du journal officiel*, no. 100, 6 December 1990, approved by the Académie française.

Al Lawati, Abbas. 2011. During the Arab Media Forum, Dubai: Social Media Played Role in Facilitating Arab Spring. *Media in Egypt*, 18 May. www.mediainegypt.com/2011/05/social-media-played-role-in.html.

American Bar Association. 1999. Plain Language Resolution 9–10 August 1999. www.plainlanguage.gov/populartopics/regulations/aba.cfm.

Anand, Chetan. n.d. Writing Punjabi using the Roman Alphabet. www.scribd.com/doc/43452449/Punjabi-and-Roman-Characters.

Andrews, Carol, and Stephen Quirke. 1988. *The Rosetta Stone: Facsimile Drawing*. London: The British Museum Press.

Angheli, Natalia. 2003. Moldova. In A. Karlsreiter (ed.) *Media in Multilingual Societies: Freedom and Responsibility*. Vienna: OECD, 71–94.

ANLCI. 2005. Agence Nationale de Lutte contre l'illettrisme. L'enquête IVQ 2004–2005. http://anlci.gouv.fr/?id=445.

Arnold, Robert W., and Beth T. Nakatsui. 2010. *American Sign Language Writing*. North Hollywood, CA: Digits and Digibet. www.si5s.com.

Artico, Francesco. 1976. *Tornén un pas indrìo: raccolta di conversazioni in dialetto*. Brescia: Paideia Editrice.

Assmann, Jan. 1991. *Stein und Zeit: Mensch und Gesellschaft im alten Ägypten*. Munich: Wilhelm Fink Verlag.

Auerbach, Elsa. 1992. Literacy and Ideology. *Annual Review of Applied Linguistics* 12, 71–85.

Backhaus, Peter. 2007. *Linguistic Landscapes: A Comparative Study of Urban Multilingualism in Tokyo*. Clevedon: Multilingual Matters.

Ball, Arnetha F. and Ted Lardner. 2005. *African American Literacies Unleashed: Vernacular English and the Composition Classroom*. Carbondale, IL: Southern Illinois University Press.

155

Baron, Dennis. 2009. *A Better Pen: Readers, Writers, and the Digital Revolution.* Oxford University Press.

Baron, Naomi S. 2008. *Always On: Language in an Online and Mobile World.* Oxford University Press.

Barton, David. 1994. The social impact of literacy. In Ludo Verhoeven (ed.) *Functional Literacy: Theoretical Issues and Educational Applications.* Amsterdam, Philadelphia: John Benjamins, 185–97.

Barton, David, and Uta Papen. 2010. *The Anthropology of Writing: Understanding Textually Mediated Worlds.* London: Continuum.

Becker-Cantarino, Barbara. 1988. *Low German as a Literary Language in Schlesweg-Holstein in the Seventeenth Century.* Berlin: DeGruyter.

Bell, Allan. 2001. Back in Style: Reworking Audience Design. In P. Eckert and J. R. Rickford (eds.) *Style and Sociolinguistic Variation.* Cambridge and New York: Cambridge University Press, 139–69.

Bell, Masha 2004. *Understanding English Spelling.* Cambridge: Pegasus Elliot MacKenzie.

Bell, Richard. 1937. *The Quran Translated with a Critical Rearrangement of the Surahs.* Edinburgh: T. & T. Clark.

Ben-Rafael, Eliezer. 2009. A Sociological Approach to the Study of Linguistic Landscapes. In Elana Shohamy and Durk Gorter (eds.) *Linguistic Landscape: Expanding the Scenery.* New York and London: Routledge, 40–54.

Bergs, Alexander. 2005. *Social Networks and Historical Sociolinguistics.* Berlin, New York: Mouton de Gruyter.

Bernstein, Basil. 1962. Social Class, Linguistic Codes and Grammatical Elements. *Language and Speech* 5, 221–40.

1966. Elaborated and Restricted Codes: An Outline. *Sociological Inquiry* 36, 254–61.

1971. *Class, Codes and Control,* Vol. I. London: Routledge and Kegan Paul.

Beswick, Jaine E. 2007. *Regional Nationalism in Spain: Language Use and Ethnic Identity in Galicia.* Clevedon: Multilingual Matters.

Biber, Douglas. 1988. *Variation across Speech and Writing.* Cambridge University Press.

Biber, Douglas, and Susan Conrad. 2009. *Register, Genre, and Style.* Cambridge University Press.

Blair, Sheila. 2008. *Islamic Calligraphy.* Edinburgh University Press.

Blanche-Benveniste, Claire. 1994. The Construct of Oral and Written Language. In Ludo Verhoeven (ed.) *Functional Literacy: Theoretical Issues and Educational Applications.* Amsterdam, Philadelphia: John Benjamins, 61–74.

Bloomfield, Leonard. 1933. *Language.* New York: Holt, Rinehart and Winston.

Bourdieu, Pierre. 1977. L'économie des échanges linguistiques. *Langue Française* 34, 17–34.

1982. *Ce que parler veut dire.* Paris: Fayard.

1984. *Distinction: A Social Critique of the Judgment of Taste,* trans. R. Nice. Cambridge, MA: Harvard University Press.

1991. *Language and Symbolic Power*, trans. G. Raymond and M. Adamson. Cambridge, MA: Harvard University Press.

Britto, Francis. 1986. *Diglossia: A Study of the Theory with Application to Tamil*. Washington, DC: Georgetown University Press.

Broadbrige, Judith. 2000. The Ethnolinguistic Vitality of Alsatian-speakers in Southern Alsace. In S. Wolff (ed.) *German Minorities in Europe*. Bern: Peter Lang, 47–62.

Burgess, Anthony. 1992. *A Mouthful of Air: Language and Languages, Especially English*. London: Hutchinson.

Burns, Alfred. 1981. Athenian Literacy in the Fifth Century B.C. *Journal of the History of Ideas* 42(3), 371–87.

Calhoun, Craig. 1989. Revolution and Repression in Tiananmen Square. *Sociology* 26, 21–38.

2002. Imagining Solidarity: Cosmopolitanism, Constitutional Patriotism, and the Public Sphere. *Public Culture* 14, 147–72.

2003. Information Technology and the International Public Sphere. In Douglas Schuler and Peter Day (eds.) *Shaping the Network Society: The New Role of Civil Society in Cyberspace*. Cambridge, MA: MIT Press, 229–51.

Calvet, Louis-Jean. 1987. *La guerre des langues et les politiques linguistiques*. Paris: Payot.

1990. Des mots sur les murs: une comparaison entre Paris et Dakar. In R. Chaudenson (ed.) *Des langues et des villes. Actes du colloque international à Dakar, du 15 au 17 décembre 1990*. Paris: Agence de coopération culturelle et technique, 73–83.

Cardona, Giorgio R. 2009. *Introduzione alla sociolinguistica*, ed. Glauco Sanga. Milan: UTET Università.

Carlson, Keith Thor, Kristina Fagan and Natalia Khaneko-Friesen (eds.). 2010. *Orality and Literacy: Reflections across Disciplines*. Toronto University Press.

Carney, Edward. 1994. *A Survey of English Spelling*. London: Routledge.

Cenoz, Jasone, and Durk Gorter. 2006. Linguistic Landscape and Minority Languages. *International Journal of Multilingualism* (special issue) 3(1), 67–80.

Chen, Ping. 1996. Toward a Phonographic Writing System of Chinese: A Case Study in Writing Reform. *International Journal of the Sociology of Language* 122, 1–46.

Chomsky, Noam, and Morris Halle. 1968. *The Sound Pattern of English*. New York: Harper and Row.

Citron, Abraham F. 1981. Our Spelling: Pride, Prudery and Waste. *The Urban Review* 13(3), 181–8.

Civil, Miguel. 1995. Ancient Mesopotamian Lexicography. In Jack M. Sasson (ed.) *Civilizations of the Ancient Near East*. New York: Charles Scribner's Sons, 2305–14.

Clanchy, Michael T. 1979. *From Memory to Written Record in England, 1066–1307*. Cambridge, MA: Harvard University Press.

Clarity. 2002. *A Movement to Simplify Legal Language* 47, May 2002. www. clarity-international.net/journals/47.pdf.

Clement, Victoria. 2008. Emblems of Independence: Script Choice in Post-Soviet Turkmenistan. *International Journal of the Sociology of Language* 192, 171–85.

Code of Hammurabi. 1904. Trans. and ed. with glossary and index of subjects, by Robert Francis Harper. University of Chicago Press.

Coluzzi, Paolo. 2007. *Minority Language Planning and Micronationalism in Italy.* Bern: Peter Lang.

Cook, Vivian, and Benedetta Bassetti (eds.). 2005. *Second Language Writing Systems.* Clevedon, Buffalo, Toronto: Multilingual Matters.

Corbett, Edward P. 1981. The Status of Writing in our Society. In M. Farr Whiteman (ed.) *Writing: The Nature, Development and Teaching of Written Communication*, Vol. I. Hillsdale, NJ: Lawrence Erlbaum, 47–52.

Corley, Mary Ann. 2003. Poverty, Racism and Literacy. ERIC Educational Reports. http://findarticles.com/p/articles/mi_pric/is_200300/ai_3805607591/?tag=content;col1.

Cossu, Giuseppe. 1999. The Acquisition of Italian Orthography. In M. Harris and G. Hatano (eds.) *Learning to Read and Write: A Cross-Linguistic Perspective.* Cambridge University Press, 10–33.

Coulmas, Florian. 1983. Writing and Literacy in China. In Florian Coulmas and Konrad Ehlich (eds.) *Writing in Focus.* Berlin: Mouton, 239–53.

(ed.). 1984. *Linguistic Minorities and Literacy: Language Policy Issues in Developing Countries.* Berlin: Mouton.

1992. *Language and Economy.* Oxford: Blackwell.

1994. Writing Systems and Literacy: The Alphabetic Myth Revisited. In Ludo Verhoeven (ed.) *Functional Literacy: Theoretical Issues and Educational Implications.* Amsterdam, Philadelphia: John Benjamins, 305–20.

1996. *The Blackwell Encyclopaedia of Writing Systems.* Oxford: Blackwell.

1998. Spelling with a Capital S. *Written Language and Literacy* 1 (2), 249–52.

2002. Writing is Crucial. *International Journal of the Sociology of Language* 157, 59–62.

2003. *Writing Systems: An Introduction to Their Linguistic Analysis.* Cambridge University Press.

2005. *Sociolinguistics: The Study of Speakers' Choices.* Cambridge, New York, Melbourne: Cambridge University Press.

2009. Language and Economy. In Li Wei and Vivian Cook (eds.) *Contemporary Applied Linguistics*, Vol. II: *Linguistics for the Real World.* London: Continuum, 28–45.

Creppell, Ingrid. 1989. Democracy and Literacy: The Role of Culture in Political Life. *Archives Européennes de Sociologie* 30, 22–47.

Cressy, David. 1980. *Literacy and the Social Order: Reading and Writing in Tudor and Stuart England.* Cambridge University Press.

Crystal, David. 2001. *Language and the Internet.* Cambridge University Press.

2008. *Txtng: The gr8 db8.* Oxford University Press.

Curran, Brian A., Anthony Grafton, Pamela O. Long and Benjamin Weiss. 2009. *Obelisk: A History*. Cambridge, MA: MIT Press.

Danet, Brenda, and Susan C. Herring. 2007. *The Multilingual Internet*. Oxford University Press.

Daniels, Peter T. 2008. Grammatology. In D. R. Olson and N. Torrance (eds.) *The Cambridge Handbook of Literacy*. Cambridge University Press, 25–45.

Danzig, Arnold. 1995. Applications and Distortions of Basil Bernstein's Code Theory. In A. R. Sadovnik (ed.) *Knowledge and Pedagogy: The Sociology of Basil Bernstein*. Norwood, NJ: Ablex, 145–69.

Daswani, C. J. (ed.). 2001. *Language Education in Multilingual India*. New Delhi: UNESCO.

Davis, William S. (ed.). 1912–13. *Readings in Ancient History: Illustrative Extracts from the Sources*, 2 vols. Boston: Allyn and Bacon.

D'Avray, David L. 2010. *Rationalities in History*. Cambridge University Press.

De Biasi, Pierre-Marc. 1999. *Le papier: une aventure au quotidien*. Paris: Gallimard.

DeFrancis, John. 1950. *Nationalism and Language Reform in China*. Princeton University Press.

Del Valle, José, and Laura Villa. 2006. Spanish in Brazil: Language Policy, Business, and Cultural Propaganda. *Language Policy* 5, 369–92.

 2012. La disputada autoridad de las academias: debate lingüístico-ideológico en torno a la *Ortografía* de 2010. *Revista Internacional de Lingüística Iberoamericana (RILI)* 19.

Derrida, Jacques. 1967. *De la grammatologie*. Paris: Éditions de Minuit [*Of Grammatology*, trans. Gayatri Chakravorty Spivak. Baltimore: The Johns Hopkins University Press, 1974].

 1972. *Positions*. Paris: Éditions Minuit.

Deshpande, Madhav M. 1979. *Sociolinguistic Attitudes in India: A Historical Reconstruction*. Ann Arbor, MI: Karoma.

Deumert, Ana. 2004. *Language Standardization and Language Change: The Dynamics of Cape Dutch*. Amsterdam: John Benjamins.

Dighe, Anita. 2000. The Role of Adult Education in Reducing Class and Gender Disparities. In C. J. Daswani and S. Y. Shah (eds.) *Adult Education in India*. New Delhi: UNESCO, 321–30.

Djité, Paulin. 2008. Development and the National Language Question: A Case Study. *International Journal of the Sociology of Language*, 212, 43–54.

 2011. *The Sociolinguistics of Development in Africa*. Clevedon: Multilingual Matters.

Donati, Angela. 2002. *Epigraphia romana: la communicazione nell'antichità*. Bologna: Il Molino.

Dufour, Philippe. 2009. Lire: écrire. Flaubert. *Revue Critique et Génétique* 2. http://flaubert.revues.org/845.

EBLUL-France, The French Committee of the European Bureau for Lesser-used Languages. 2007. Regional and Minority Languages and Cultures in France are Outlaws, a paper addressed to the UN Committee on

Economic, Social and Cultural Rights. www2.ohchr.org/english/bodies/ cescr/docs/info-ngos/eblul.pdf.

Eckkrammer, Eva. M., and Hildgrun M. Eder. 2000. *(Cyber)Diskurs zwischen Konvention und Revolution. Eine multilinguale textlinguistische Analyse von Gebrauchstextsorten im realen und virtuellen Raum.* (Studien zur romanischen Sprachwissenschaft und interkulturellen Kommunikation 2.) Frankfurt am Main: Peter Lang.

Eisenstein, Elizabeth L. 1979. *The Printing Press as an Agent of Change.* Cambridge University Press.

Elley, Warwick B. 1993. *Reading: Literacy in Thirty Countries.* Oxford: Pergamon.

Eroms, Hans-Werner, and Horst Haider Munske (eds.). 1997. *Die Rechtschreibreform. Pro und Kontra.* Berlin: Erich Schmidt Verlag.

Extra, Guus, and Ludo Verhoeven. 1992. *Immigrant Languages in Europe.* Clevedon: Multilingual Matters.

Falkenstein, Adam. 1954. La cité – temple sumérienne. *Cahier d'Histoire Mondiale* (Neuchâtel) 1, 784–814.

Febvre, Lucien, and Henri-Jean Martin. 1999 [1958]. *L'apparition du livre.* Paris: Albin Michel (Bibliothèque Évolution Humanité).

Ferguson, Charles A. 1959. Diglossia. *Word* 15, 325–40.

Ferguson, Ronnie. 2007. *A Linguistic History of Venice.* Florence: Leo S. Olschki.

Fischer, Hervé. 2006. *Digital Shock: Confronting the New Reality.* Montreal: McGill-Queen's University Press.

Fisher, J. H. 1977. Chancery and the Emergence of Standard Written English in the Fifteenth Century. *Speculum* 52, 870–99.

Fishman, Joshua A. 1967. Bilingualism With and Without Diglossia: Diglossia With and Without Bilingualism. *Journal of Social Issues* 23, 29–38.

 1988. Ethnocultural Issues in the Creation, Substitution, and Revision of Writing Systems. In Bennett A. Rafoth and Donald L. Rubin (eds.) *The Social Construction of Written Communication.* Norwood NJ: Ablex, 273–86.

 1991. *Reversing Language Shift.* Clevedon: Multilingual Matters.

Fiske, John. 2002. *Introduction to Communication Studies.* London: Routledge.

Fodor, István, and Claude Hagège (eds.). 1983–90. *Language Reform, History and Future,* 3 vols. Hamburg: Buske.

François, Alexis. 1959. *Histoire de la langue Française cultivée: des origins à nos jours.* Geneva: Jullien.

Frangoudaki, Anna. 2002. Greek Societal Bilingualism of More Than a Century. *International Journal of the Sociology of Language* 157, 101–7.

Freedman, Adam. 2007. *The Party of the First Part: The Curious World of Legalese.* New York: Henry Holt.

Fromkin, Victoria. 2000. *Linguistics: An Introduction.* Malden, MA: Blackwell.

Gair, James W. 1986. Sinhala Diglossia Revisited *or* Diglossia Dies Hard. In Bh. Krishnamurti, C. Masica and A. K. Sinha (eds.) *South Asian Languages: Structure, Convergence and Diglossia.* Delhi: Motilal Banarsidass, 322–36.

Gao Liwei. 2008. Language Change in Progress: Evidence from Computer Mediated Communication. In Marjorie K. M. Chan and Haria Kang (eds.) *Proceedings of the 20th North American Conference on Chinese Linguistics (NACCL-20)* . Columbus: The Ohio State University, Vol. I, 361–77.

Gardner, Rod, Richard Fitzgerald and Ilana Mushin. 2009. The Underlying Orderliness in Turn-taking. *Australian Journal of Communication* 36(3), 65–89. http://aiemca.net/wp-content/uploads/2010/01/Orderliness.pdf.

Garner, Bryan. 1995. *A Dictionary of Modern Legal Usage*. Oxford University Press.

Garnham, Nicholas. 2000. The Role of the Public Sphere in the Information Society. In C. T. Marsden (eds.) *Regulating the Global Information Society*. London: Routledge, 43–56.

Gee, James P. 1990. *Social Linguistics and Literacies: Ideology in Discourses. Critical Perspectives on Literacy and Education*. London: Falmer Press.

2005. *An Introduction to Discourse Analysis: Theory and Method*. London: Routledge.

Gelb, I. J. 1963. *A Study of Writing*. Chicago and London: University of Chicago Press.

Gerö, Eva-Carin, and Hans Ruge. 2008. Continuity and Change. The History of Two Greek Tenses. In Folke Josephson and Ingmar Söhrman (eds.) *Interdependence of Diachronic and Synchronic Analysis*. Amsterdam, Philadelphia: John Benjamins, 105–29.

Ghose, Malini. 2001. Women and Empowerment through Literacy. In D. Olson and N. Torrance (eds.) *The Making of Literate Societies*. Oxford: Blackwell, 296–316.

Giles, Howard, and Nikolas Coupland. 1991. *Language: Contexts and Consequences*. Milton Keynes: Open University Press.

Goethe-Wörterbuch. N.d. www.uni-tuebingen.de/gwb/.

Goody, Jack. 1977. *The Domestication of the Savage Mind*. Cambridge University Press.

1987. *The Logic of Writing and the Organization of Society*. Cambridge University Press.

Goody, Jack, and Ian Watt. 1968. The Consequences of Literacy. In Jack Goody (ed.) *Literacy in Traditional Societies*. Cambridge University Press, 27–68.

Gorter, Durk (ed.). 2006. Linguistic Landscape: A New Approach to Multilingualism. *International Journal of Multilingualism* (special issue).

Gottlieb, Nanette. 2011. Technology and the Writing System in Japan. In P. Heinrich and C. Galan (eds.) *Language Life in Japan: Transformations and Prospects*. London and New York: Routledge, 140–53.

Graff, Harvey J. 1986. The History of Literacy: Toward the Third Generation. *Interchange* 17(2), 122–34.

Green, Richard Firth. 1999. *A Crisis of Truth: Literature and Law in Ricardian England*. Philadelphia: University of Pennsylvania Press, 1999.

Grillo, Ralph D. 1989. *Dominant Languages: Language and Hierarchy in Britain and France*. Cambridge University Press.

Guérin-Pace, F., and A. Blum. 1999. L'illusion comparative: les logiques d'élaboration et d'utilisation d'une enquête internationale sur l'illettrisme. *Population* 54, 271–302.

Guerini, Federica. 2006. *Language Alternation Strategies in a Multilingual Setting: A Sociolinguistic Study of Ghanaian Immigrants in Northern Italy*. Bern: Peter Lang.

Habermas, Jürgen. 1991 [1962]. *The Structural Transformation of the Public Sphere: An Inquiry into a Category of Bourgeois Society*, trans. Thomas Berger, with the assistance of Frederick Lawrence. Cambridge, MA: MIT Press [*Strukturwandel der Öffentlichkeit. Untersuchungen zu einer Kategorie der bürgerlichen Gesellschaft*. Frankfurt: Suhrkamp].

    1974. The Public Sphere: An Encyclopedia Article (1964). *New German Critique* 3, 49–55.

    2008. Public Space and Political Public Sphere: The Biographical Roots of Two Motifs in my Thought. In *Habermas Between Naturalism and Religion: Philosophical Essays*. Polity, 11–23.

Haeri, Niloofar. 2003. *Sacred Language, Ordinary People*. New York: Palgrave

Halliday, M. A. K. 1985. *Spoken and Written Language*. Oxford University Press.

Harris, Roy. 1980. *The Language Makers*. Ithaca, NY: Cornell University Press.

    1986. *The Origin of Writing*. London: Duckworth.

    2000. *Rethinking Writing*. London: Athlon Press.

Harris, William V. 1989. *Ancient Literacy*. Cambridge, MA: Harvard University Press.

Hartley, John. 2009. *The Uses of Digital Literacy*. St Lucia, Qld.: University of Queensland Press.

Harvey, F. D. 1966. Literacy in Athenian Democracy. *Revue des Études Grecques* 79, 585–635.

Hatcher, Lynley, 2008. Script Change in Azerbaijan: Acts of Identity. *International Journal of the Sociology of Language* 192, 105–16.

Havelock, Eric A. 1982. *The Literate Revolution in Greece and its Cultural Consequences*. Princeton University Press.

Haviland, John B. 2006. Documenting Lexical Knowledge. In J. Gippert, N. P. Himmelmann and U. Mosel (eds.) *Essentials of Language Documentation*. Berlin, New York: Mouton DeGruyter, 129–62.

Heath, Shirley. B. 1981. Toward an Ethnohistory of Writing in American Education. In M. Farr Whiteman (ed.) *Writing: The Nature, Development and Teaching of Written Communication*, Vol. I. Hillsdale, NJ: Lawrence Erlbaum, 25–45.

    1982. Protean Shapes in Literacy Events: Ever-shifting Oral and Literate Traditions. In D. Tannen (ed.) *Spoken and Written Language: Exploring Orality and Literacy*. Norwood, NJ: Ablex, 91–117.

Heller, Monica. 2001. Legitimate Language in a Multilingual School. In M. Heller and M. Martin-Jones (eds.) *Voices of Authority: Education and Linguistic Difference*. Westport, CT: Ablex, 381–402.

2003. Globalization, the New Economy, and the Commodification of Language and Identity. *Journal of Sociolinguistics* 7(4), 473–92.

Hilali, M. T. al-, and M. M. Kan. 1983. *Translation of the Meaning of the Noble Qur'an in The English Language*. Medina, Saudi Arabia: King Fahd Complex.

Hilbert, Martin, and Priscila López. 2011. The World's Technological Capacity to Store, Communicate, and Compute Information. *Science* 332, 60–5.

Himmelmann, Nikolaus P. 2006. The Challenges of Segmenting Spoken Language. In J. Gippert, N. P. Himmelmann and U. Mosel (eds.) *Essentials of Language Documentation*. Berlin, New York: Mouton DeGruyter, 253–74.

Hopkins, Jason. 2008. Choosing How to Write Sign Language: A Sociolinguistic Perspective. *International Journal of the Sociology of Language* 192, 75–89.

Howley, Kevin. 2005. *Community Media: People, Places and Communication Technologies*. London: Cambridge University Press.

Hudson, Alan. 2002. Outline of a Theory of Diglossia. *International Journal of the Sociology of Language* 157, 1–48.

Indigenous Literacy Project. n.d. www.indigenousliteracyproject.org.au/About/IndigenousLiteracy.aspx.

Jaffe, Alexandra. 2000. Non-standard Orthography and Non-standard Speech. *Journal of Sociolinguistics* 4, 497–513.

Jama, Deeqa, and George Dugdale. 2010. Literacy: State of the Nation. A Picture of Literacy in the UK Today. National Literacy Trust. www.literacytrust.org.uk/assets/0000/3816/FINAL_Literacy_State_of_the_Nation_-_30_March_2010.pdf.

Jeffrey, David L. 1996. *People of the Book: Christian Identity and Literary Culture*. Grand Rapids, MI: Wm B. Eerdmans.

Jencks, Christopher, and Meridith Phillips (eds.). 1998. *The Black–White Test Score Gap*. Washington, DC: The Brookings Institute.

Johnson, Sally. 2003. The Cultural Politics of the 1998 Reform of German Orthography. *German Life and Letters* 53, 106–25.

Jones, Derek (ed.). 2001. *Censorship: A World Encyclopedia*, Vols. I –IV. London: Fitzroy Dearborn.

Kahane, Henry. 1986. A Typology of the Prestige Language. *Language* 62, 495–508.

Kalantzis, Mary, and Bill Cope (eds.). 2000. *Multiliteracies and the Design of Social Futures*. Abingdon: Routledge.

Kasapi, Eleni. 2009. Viral Advertising: Internet Entertainment and Virtual Society. In H. Powell *et al.* (eds.) *The Advertising Handbook*. London and New York: Routledge, 119–25.

Kaye, Alan S. 2002. Comment on Alan Hudson's 'Outline of a Theory of Diglossia'. *International Journal of the Sociology of Language* 157, 117–25.

Kemp, Nenagh. 2010. Texting versus Txtng: Reading and Writing Text Messages, and Links with Other Linguistic Skills. *Writing Systems Research* 2, 53–71.

Kim-Renaud, Young-Key (ed.). 1997. *The Korean Alphabet: Its History and Structure*. Honolulu: University of Hawaii Press.

Kimble, J. 1995. Answering the Critics of Plain Language. *The Scribes Journal of Legal Writing* 5, 51–85.

Kloss, Heinz. 1967. Abstand Languages and Ausbau Languages. *Anthropological Linguistics* 9, 29–41.

Koller, Andreas. 2010. The Public Sphere and Comparative Historical Research. *Social Science History* 34(3), 261–90.

Krishnamurti, Bh. (ed.). 1986. *South Asian Languages: Structure, Convergence and Diglossia*. Delhi: Motilal Banarsidass.

Krumbacher, Karl. 1902. *Das Problem der neugriechischen Schriftsprache*. Munich: Königlich-Bayrische Akademie.

Labov, William. 1969. The Logic of Non-Standard English. In J. Alatis (ed.) *Georgetown Monographs on Languages and Linguistics 22*. Washington, DC: Georgetown University Press, 1–44.

   1972. *Sociolinguistic Patterns*. Philadelphia: University of Pennsylvania Press.

   1994. *Principles of Linguistic Change*. Blackwell.

Landry, Rodrigue, and Richard Y. Bourhis. 1997. Linguistic Landscape and Ethnolinguistic Vitality. *Journal of Language and Social Psychology* 16(1), 23–49.

Lartichaux, Jean-Yves. 1977. Linguistic Politics during the French Revolution. *Diogenes* 97, 65–84.

Lawton, Denis. 1968. *Social Class, Language and Education*. London: Routledge and Kegan Paul.

Lee, Alison. 1996. *Gender, Literacy, Curriculum: Re-writing School Geography*. Milton Park, Abingdon: Taylor and Francis.

Leech, Geoffrey (with D. Biber, S. Johansson, S. Conrad and E. Finegan). 1999. *Longman Grammar of Spoken and Written English*. London: Longman.

Lehtonen, Annukka. 2005. Sources of Information Children use in Learning to Spell: The Case of Finnish Geminates. In R. Malathesa Joshi and P. G. Aaron (eds.) *Handbook of Orthography and Literacy*. Mahwah, NJ: Lawrence Erlbaum, 63–79.

Leibniz, Gottfried. 1680. Préceptes pour avançer les sciences [*Leibniz: Selections*, ed. Philip P. Wiener. New York: Charles Scribner's Sons, 1951, 29–46].

leo. – Level-One Studie. 2011. Hamburg University. http://blogs.epb.uni-hamburg.de/leo/files/2011/02/leo-Presseheft-web.pdf.

Lévi-Strauss, Claude. 1973[1955]. *Tristes tropiques*. trans. J. & D. Weightman. London: Cape. [*Tristes Tropiques*. Paris: Plon].

Levine, Kenneth. 1994. Functional Literacy in a Changing World. In Ludo Verhoeven (ed.) *Functional Literacy: Theoretical Issues and Educational Applications*. Amsterdam, Philadelphia: John Benjamins, 113–31.

Lewis, Geoffrey. 2002. *The Turkish Language Reform: A Catastrophic Success.* Oxford University Press.

Lewis, Mark Edward. 1999. *Writing and Authority in Early China.* SUNY Series in Chinese Philosophy and Culture. Albany: State University of New York Press.

Linell, Per. 2005. *The Written Language Bias in Linguistics: Its Nature, Origin and Transformation.* London: Routledge.

Lo Bianco, Joseph. 2000. Multiliteracies and Multilingualism. In Bill Cope and Mary Kalantzis (eds.) *Multiliteracies: Literacy Learning and the Design of Social Futures.* Abingdon: Routledge, 92–105.

Luther, Martin. 1529. Eine Heerpredigt wider die Türken [Military Sermon Against the Turks]. *Weimarer Ausgabe (WA)* 53, 272–396.

    1530. Sendbrief vom Dolmetschen [Open Letter on Translating]. *Weimarer Ausgabe (WA)* 7, 544–604 [English translation by Gary Mann. www.iclnet. org/pub/resources/text/wittenberg/luther/luther-translate.txt].

Lyons, John. 1968. *Introduction to Theoretical Linguistics.* Cambridge University Press.

Maksymiuk, Jan. 1999. An Orthography on Trial in Belarus. *Written Language and Literacy* 2(1), 141–4.

Marfany, Joan-Lluís. 2010. Sociolinguistics and Some of its Concepts. *International Journal of the Sociology of Language* 206, 1–20.

Marshall, David F. 2011. The Reforming of English Spelling. In J. A. Fishman and O. García (eds.) *Handbook of Language and Ethnic Identity*, Vol. II. Oxford, New York: Oxford University Press, 113–25.

Martin-Jones, Marilyn, and Kathryn Jones. 2000. *Multilingual Literacies: Reading and Writing Different Worlds.* Amsterdam, Philadelphia: John Benjamins.

Matthews, P. H. 2003. *Linguistics: A Very Short Introduction.* Oxford University Press.

McGuigan, Jim. 1996. *Culture and the Public Sphere.* London and New York: Routledge.

McKee, Alan. 2005. *The Public Sphere: An Introduction.* Cambridge University Press.

Mellikoff, David. 1992. *Mellikof's Dictionary of American Legal Usage.* St Paul: West Publishing Co.

Michel, Jean-Baptiste, *et al.* 2010. Quantitative Analysis of Culture Using Millions of Digitized Books. *Science.* www.sciencexpress.org/ 16 December 2010/10.1126/science.1199644.

Morris, Ian. 2010. *Why the West Rules – For Now.* New York: Farrar, Straus and Giroux.

Moss, Gemma. 2007. *Literacy and Gender: Researching Texts, Contexts and Readers.* Milton Park, Abingdon: Routledge.

Movement for Canadian Literacy. n.d. *Literacy for Life, Fact Sheet #9.* www.nald. ca/library/research/mcl/factsht/poverty/page1.htm.

Müller, Karin. 1990. *'Schreibe, wie du sprichst!' Eine Maxime im Spannungsfeld von Mündlichkeit und Schriftlichkeit.* Frankfurt am Main, Bern, New York: Peter Lang.

Negroponte, Nicholas. 1995. *Being Digital.* New York: Alfred A. Knopf. (A cyberspace extension at http://archives.obs-us.com/obs/english/books/nn/bdintro.htm.)

Neidhardt, Friedhelm. 1994. Öffentlichkeit, öffentliche Meinung, soziale Bewegungen. In Friedhelm Neidhardt (ed.) *Öffentlichkeit, öffentliche Meinung, soziale Bewegungen.* Opladen: Westdeutscher Verlag, 7–41.

Nystrand, Martin. 1986. *The Structure of Written Communication.* Orlando, FL: Academic Press.

O'Grady, William, Michael Dobrovoesky and Francis Katamba. 1997. *Contemporary Linguistics: An Introduction.* London: Longman.

O'Keef, Barbara J., and Jesse G. Delia. 1988. Communicative Tasks and Communicative Practices: The Development of Audience-centered Message Production. In Bennett A. Rafoth and Donald L. Rubin (eds.) *The Social Construction of Written Communication.* Norwood, NJ: Ablex, 70–98.

OECD. 1996. *The Knowledge-Based Economy.* Paris: OECD: OECD/GD (96) 102.

1997. *Literacy Skills for the Knowledge Society: Further Results from the International Adult Literacy Survey.* Paris: OECD.

2000. *Literacy in the Information Age: Final Report of the International Adult Literacy Survey.* Paris: OECD.

Olson, David R. 1977. From Utterance to Text: The Bias of Language in Speech and Writing. *Harvard Educational Review* 47(3), 257–86.

1994. *The World on Paper.* Cambridge University Press.

Olson, David R., and Nancy Torrance (eds.). 1991. *Literacy and Orality.* Cambridge University Press.

Omoniyi, Tope. 2010. Introduction: Change, Accommodation and Conflict. In Tope Omoniyi (ed.) *The Sociology of Language and Religion.* New York: Palgrave Macmillan, 1–13.

Ong, Walter J. 1982. *Orality and Literacy: The Technologizing of the Word.* London: Methuen.

Pandharipande, Rajeshwari. 1992. Language and Religion in South Asia: The Case of Hindi. In Edward C. Dimock, Braj B. Kachru and Bh. Krishnamurti (eds.) *Dimensions of Sociolinguistics in South Asia.* New Delhi: Oxford & IBH Publishing Co., 271–83.

Parkinson, Richard. 1999. *Cracking Codes: The Rosetta Stone and Decipherment.* London: British Museum Press.

Philipsen, Gerry. 1997. A Theory of Speech Codes. In G. Philipsen and T. L. Albrecht (eds.) *Developing Communication Theories.* Albany: State University of New York Press, 119–56.

Pitman, K. B. E., Sir James, and John StJohn. 1969. *Alphabets and Reading.* London: Pitman.

Poole, Stuart C. 1999. *An Introduction to Linguistics.* Houndmills: Palgrave Macmillan.

Posener, Georges. 1956. *Littérature et politique dans l'Égypte de la XIIe dynastie.* (Bibliothèque de l'École des hautes études, 2007.) Paris: Honoré Champion.

Premi, Mahendra K. 2002. India's Literacy Panorama. Seminar on Progress of Literacy in India: What the Census 2001 Reveals. New Delhi: NIPA, 5 October 2002. www.educationforallinindia.com/page172.html.

Radford, Andrew, Martin Atkinson, David Britain, Harald Clahsen and Andrew Spencer. 1999. *Linguistics: An Introduction.* Cambridge University Press.

Randall, Neil. 2002. Lingo Online. A Report on the Language of the Keyboard Generation. www.arts.uwaterloo.ca/~nrandall/LingoOnline-finalreport.pdf.

Redd, Teresa, and Karen Schuster. 2005. *A Teacher's Introduction to African American English: What a Writing Teacher Should Know.* Urbana, IL: National Council of Teachers of English.

Roberts, Celia, and Brian Street. 1997. Spoken and Written Language. In F. Coulmas (ed.) *The Handbook of Sociolinguistics.* Oxford: Blackwells, 168–86.

Rodell, Fred. 1936. Goodbye to Law Reviews. *Virginia Law Review* 23, 38–45.

Rohlfs, Jeffrey. 1974. A Theory of Interdependent Demand for a Communications Service. *Bell Journal of Economics and Management Science* 5(1), 16–37.

Rosen, Harold. 1972. *Language and Class.* Bristol: The Falling Wall Press.

Rosowsky, Andrey. 2010. 'Writing it in English': Script Choices among Young Multilingual Muslims in the UK. *Journal of Multilingual and Multicultural Development* 31, 163–79.

Sadovnik, Alan R. (ed.). 1995. *Knowledge and Pedagogy: The Sociology of Basil Bernstein.* Norwood, NJ: Ablex.

Sallabank, Julia. 2002. Writing in an Unwritten Language: The Case of Guernsey French. *Reading Working Papers in Linguistics,* 6, 217–44.

Salomon, Richard. 1998. *Indian Epigraphy: A Guide to the Study of Inscriptions in Sanskrit, Prakrit and other Indo-Aryan Languages.* New Delhi: Vedams Books.

Sassoon, Rosemary. 1995. *The Acquisition of a Second Writing System.* Intellect.

Saussure, Ferdinand de. 1978. *Course in General Linguistics,* New York: Fontana/ Collins. Trans. from the French (*Cours de linguistique générale,* 1972 [1916]) by Wade Baskin.

Schiffman, Harold. 1996. *Linguistic Culture and Language Policy.* London and New York: Routledge.

  1997. Diglossia as a Sociolinguistic Situation. In F. Coulmas (ed.) *The Handbook of Sociolinguistics.* Blackwells, 205–16.

Searle, John. 2005. Language, Writing, Mind, and Consciousness. Children of the Code. Interview with John Searle, 29 June 2005. www.childrenofthecode.org/interviews/searle.htm#Technology Modern%20Minds.

Sebba, Mark. 2007. *Spelling and Society*. Cambridge University Press.

Serpell, Robert, Linda Baker, and Susan Sonnenschein. 2005. *Becoming Literate in the City: The Baltimore Early Childhood Project*. Cambridge University Press.

Shakir, M. 1999. *The Holy Quran*. New York: Tahrike Tarsile Qur'an.

Shin, Sang-Soon, Don-Ju Lee and Hwan-Mook Lee (eds.). 1990. *Understanding Hunmin Jŏngŭm*. Seoul: Hanshin Publishing Co.

Shohamy, Elana, and Durk Gorter (eds.). 2009. *Linguistic Landscape: Expanding the Scenery*. New York and London: Routledge.

Simpson, J. 2002. Discourse and Synchronous Computer-mediated Communication: Uniting Speaking and Writing? In P. Thompson and K. S. Miller (eds.) *Unity and Diversity in Applied Linguistics*. London: Continuum, 57–71.

Smalley, William A. 1963. Writing Systems and their Characteristics. In *Orthography Studies: Articles on New Writing Systems by William A. Smalley and Others*. London: United Bible Societies, 1–17.

Snow, Donald B. 2004. *Cantonese as a Written Language: The Growth of a Written Chinese Vernacular*. London: Edward Arnold.

Sola Pool, Ithiel de. 1984. *Technologies of Freedom*. Cambridge, MA: Harvard University Press.

Soriano, James. 2011. Language, Learning, Identity, Privilege. *Manila Bulletin*, 24 August.

Sparks, Colin. 1991. Goodbye, Hildy Johnson: The Vanishing 'Serious Press'. In P. Dahlgren and C. Sparks (eds.) *Communication and Citizenship: Journalism and the Public Sphere in the New Media Age*. London and New York: Routledge, 58–74.

Spolsky, Bernard. 2010. Jewish Religious Multilingualism. In Tope Omoniyi (ed.) *The Sociology of Language and Religion*. New York: Palgrave Macmillan, 14–28.

Spolsky, Bernard, and Robert L. Cooper. 1991. *The Languages of Jerusalem*. Oxford University Press.

Statistics New Zealand. n.d. www2.stats.govt.nz/domino/external/web/nzstories.nsf/092edeb76ed5aa6bcc256afe0081d84e/2e308ada85f43864cc256b180004d7ba?OpenDocument.

Streeck, Wolfgang. 2010. *Taking Capitalism Seriously: Toward an Institutionalist Approach to Contemporary Political Economy*. MPIfG Discussion Paper 10/15. www.mpifg.de/pu/mpifg_dp/dp10–15.pdf.

Street, Brian V. 1995. *Social Literacies*. London: Longman.

Taavitsainen, Irma, Gunnel Melchers and Päivi Pahta (eds.). 2000. *Writing in Nonstandard English*. Amsterdam: John Benjamins.

Tabouret-Keller, Andrée, R. B. Le Page, Penelope Gardner-Chloros and Gabrielle Varro (eds.). 1997. *Vernacular Literacy*. Oxford University Press.

Tagliamonte, Sali A. and Derek Denis. 2008. Linguistic Ruin? LOL! Instant Messaging and Teen Language. *American Speech* 83(1), 3–34.

Tannen, Deborah. 1982. The Oral/Literate Continuum in Discourse. In D. Tannen (ed.) *Spoken and Written Language: Exploring Orality and Literacy.* Norwood, NJ: Ablex, 1–16.

Tanner, R. E. S. 2004. The Inequality of Unwritten Languages: Some Reflections on the Christian Use of the Vernacular in Eastern Africa. *Nordic Journal of African Studies* 13, 65–75.

Taylor, Insup, and M. Martin Taylor. 1995. *Writing and Literacy in Chinese, Korean and Japanese.* Amsterdam, Philadelphia: John Benjamins.

Tessarolo, Mariselda, and Gian Peder Pedrotti. 2009. Languages in the Canton of Grisons. *International Journal of the Sociology of Language* 199, 63–88.

Themistocleous, Christiana. 2010. Writing in a Non-standard Greek Variety: Romanized Cypriot Greek in Online Chat. *Writing Systems Research* 2, 155–68.

Thomas, Rosalind. 1992. *Literacy and Orality in Ancient Greece.* Cambridge University Press.

Tiersma, Peter M. 1999. *Legal Language.* Chicago and London: University of Chicago Press.

Trudgill, Peter. 1979. Standard and Non-standard Dialects in the United Kingdom: Problems and Policies. *International Journal of the Sociology of Language* 21, 9–24.

1992. *Introducing Language and Society.* London: Penguin.

Tulp, S. M. 1978. Reklame en tweetaligheid: Een onderzoek naar de geografische verspreiding van franstalige en nederlandstalige affiches in Brussel. *Taal en sociale integratie* 1, 261–88.

UNESCO. 1998. Bilingual Literacy and Reproductive Health. www.unesco.org/uil/litbase/?menu=4&programme=38.

2008. *Improving the Quality of Mother Tongue-Based Literacy and Learning: Case Studies from Asia, Africa and South America.* Bangkok: UNESCO.

UNESCO Institute for Statistics. 2006. http://portal.unesco.org/education/en/ev.php-URL_ID=40338&URL_DO=DO_TOPIC&URL_SECTION=201.html.

2010a. Global Education Digest 2010: Comparing Education Statistics Across the World. www.uis.unesco.org/template/pdf/ged/2010/GED_2010_EN.pdf.

2010b. Adult and Youth Literacy: Global Trends in Gender Parity. *UIS Fact Sheet, September 2010, No. 3.* www.uis.unesco.org/FactSheets/Documents/Fact_Sheet_2010_Lit_EN.pdf.

Unger, J. Marshall. 1996. *Literacy and Script Reform in Occupation Japan.* New York, Oxford: Oxford University Press.

United Nations. 1995. *The Global Platform for Action from the UN Fourth World Conference on Women.* New York: United Nations.

Unseth, Peter. 2005. Sociolinguistic Parallels between Choosing Scripts and Languages. *Written Language and Literacy* 8(1), 19–42.

van der Sijs, Nicoline. 2004. *Taal als Mensenwerk. Het Ontstaan van het ABN.* Den Haag: Sdu Uitgevers.

van der Westen, Monique. 1994. Literacy Education and Gender: The Case of Honduras. In Ludo Verhoeven (ed.) *Functional Literacy: Theoretical Issues and Educational Applications*. Amsterdam, Philadelphia: John Benjamins, 257–78.

Verhoeven, Ludo. 1987. *Ethnic Minority Children Acquiring Literacy*. Dordrecht: Foris.

Vinaya Texts. Trans. from the Pali by Rhys Davids and Herman Oldenberg, Part III, The Kullavagga, IV–XII. Sacred Books of the East, vol. 20 [1885]. Oxford: The Clarendon Press.

Waldron, Arthur. 1990. *The Great Wall of China: From History to Myth*. Cambridge University Press.

Wallace, Rex. 2005. *An Introduction to the Wall Inscriptions from Pompeii and Herculaneum*. Mundelein, IL: Bolchazy-Carducci Publishers.

Walters, Keith. 2003. Fergie's Prescience: The Changing Nature of Diglossia in Tunisia. *International Journal of the Society of Language* 163, 77–109.

Warner, Michael. 2002. *Publics and Counterpublics*. New York: Zone.

Webster, Noah. 1800 and after, various editions. *The American Spelling Book. Containing an easy standard of pronunciation, being the first part of a grammatical institute of the English language to which is added an appendix containing a moral catechism, and a federal catechism.* www.merrycoz.org/books/spelling/SPELLER.HTM.

Wheatman, Shannon R. and Terri R. LeClercq. 2011. Majority of Class Action Publication Notices Fail to Satisfy Rule 23 Requirements. *The Review of Litigation* 30(1).

Wiley, T. G. 1996. *Literacy and Language Diversity in the United States*. Washington, DC: Center of Applied Linguistics and Delta Systems.

Willemyns, Roland. 2003. Dutch. In A. Deumert and W. Vandenbussche (eds.) *Germanic Standardizations: Past to Present*. Amsterdam: John Benjamins, 93–125.

Willms, J. Douglas. 1997. Literacy Skills and Social Class. *Options Politiques*, July/August, 22–6.

Wolfram, Walt. 1997. Dialect in Society. In F. Coulmas (ed.) *The Handbook of Sociolinguistics*. Blackwell, 107–26.

Woods, Anya. 2004. *Medium or Message: Language and Faith in Ethnic Churches*. Clevedon: Multilingual Matters.

Yates, Frances A. 1983. The Italian Academies. In *Collected Essays*, Vol. II: *Renaissance and Reform: The Italian Contribution*. London: Routledge & Kegan Paul, 6–29.

Zhao, Shouhui, and Richard B. Baldauf, Jr. 2011. Simplifying Chinese Characters: Not a Simple Matter. In J. A. Fishman and O. García (eds.) *Handbook of Language and Ethnic Identity*, Vol. II. Oxford, New York: Oxford University Press, 168–79.

Zipf, George Kingsley. 1949. *Human Behavior and the Principle of Least Effort: An Introduction to Human Ecology*. New York: Hafner.

Index